Tales

TALES FROM THE STAGE

Rock n' Roll Insiders Share Their Tales of Life In &
Out of the Hard Rock and Heavy Metal Movement

By

Michael Toney

Tales Publishing, Inc.
Henderson, Nevada

To purchase additional copies of *Tales from the Stage, Volume 1* please visit: www.talesfromthestage.com

Leave feedback, reviews, or stay up to date on the progress of Volume #2 by "Liking" our Fan Page on Facebook!

www.facebook.com/talesfromthestage
Follow our Author on Twitter @mrtoney3

Photo credits on the back cover: Jay Reynolds taken by Henk Bosma, Steve "Lips" Kudlow taken by Dalila Kriheli, Oz Fox taken by Justin Pierce, Tim "Ripper" Owens taken by Henk Bosma, Paul Shortino taken by Michael Toney, Brian Tichy taken by Harold Mountain, Bruce Kulick taken by Nicola Ciccarone, Tracii Guns taken by Robin Watts.

Introduction

Not unlike most of you who have an interest in this book, I am first and foremost a fan of hard rock and heavy metal music. That is something we all have in common with the 15 participants interviewed for this book. All of the "fans" featured in the following pages have been part of the music industry for decades, and still consider music to be a good part, if not the biggest part, of their lives.

Before you jump into the meat of the book, here are a few words on my background. I began playing drums at age 13, and played in numerous hard rock/metal bands around Detroit in the 80s. I went to Ferris State University and earned a bachelor's degree in Hotel Management in 1990. I worked for numerous hotel companies over the last 21 years, spending the last decade in upper management including a five-year stint at the Hard Rock Hotel in Las Vegas. In late 2011, I found myself jobless. Realizing that I would have some spare time on my hands, I figured this was as good a time as any to follow my passion. The idea for the book in your hands was born around Christmas of 2011.

A couple of housekeeping notes. I researched each "fan" for many hours prior to the interview. Although the internet provided an abundance of information, some of it was inaccurate. You will note that some questions are asked where I am politely (or not so politely) told that my comment on the event(s) was wrong. I really didn't edit much to save face. You will run across these on occasion. I also didn't ask the exact same set of personal questions for everyone. Based on the answers, I kept what I felt was the most interesting or relevant responses in the book.

My goal for the reader? To feel like you know the person, and learn something about their life or career after reading each interview.

A great attempt was made to make the book easy to read and understand for everyone, including the non hard rock/metal fan, or musician. This is easier said than done - especially when a lifelong musician starts talking shop - but it's a great way to learn if you are unfamiliar with some of the terms used. It might help the new "rocker" to have access to Google or YouTube while reading.

The group of hard rock/metal fans interviewed for the book was incredibly diverse: guitar players, vocalists, drummers, a record company CEO, a hard rock/metal media personality...but, not one bass player. Rest assured this wasn't from lack of trying. Maybe Betsy Bitch said it best in her interview regarding bass players, but all of my efforts were futile. Hopefully I will have more luck with Volume #2.

Two things were made apparent during the interview process. I was previously aware of each item, but didn't realize the magnitude. People that work in the hard rock and heavy metal industry are a family. Regardless of their capacity or position, everyone knows everyone. There is much less bad blood than you would think. Also, the "Grunge" movement came close to strangling our music in the early 90s. Almost every "fan" brought this up during their interview, unsolicited.

During this process, I was often asked about my experience as a journalist, or how many people I had interviewed for previous stories or books. The answer was simple - Jay Reynolds from Malice and Metal Church was my first interview ever outside the context of college, but I think that added to the character of the book. I'm just a fan that was given an opportunity to grill some of my favorite Rock Pros for an hour or two about their life and career in the industry. All of the participants were incredibly generous with their time and told some great stories. I appreciated every one of them, and have even made some friends during the process.

But, enough with the technical stuff....It's time to go behind the curtain.

Insignificância

(fun facts that have little meaning)

There are 15 book participants. 40% are lead guitar players, 33.3% are lead vocalists, 13.3% are drummers, and 13.3% are executive/media. For the sake of this exercise, we classified Lips as a lead vocalist (also plays lead guitar for Anvil), Jeff Duncan as a lead guitarist (lead vocals for DC4), and Brian Tichy as a drummer (lead guitar for S.U.N.)

33.3% of the book's participants regularly smoke cigarettes. Of the smokers, 80% are lead guitar players.

Including non-biological children (documented), all participants combined have 18 kids, or an average of 1.2 kids per participant. 40% of the participants have no kids.

Regarding the 2012 U.S. Presidential Election: Presently, 4 participants are not registered to vote (2 are not U.S. citizens). Of those registered, 18% are voting Democrat, 27% are voting Republican, and 55% are undecided.

66.6% of the book's participants have at least one tattoo. 100% of the book's lead vocalists have at least one tattoo.

85.7% of the book's participants believe that marijuana should be legalized. (One participant was not asked this question).

46.6% of the book's participants are legally married. 75% of the book's lead vocalists are married, whereas only 28.5% of the book's lead guitar players are married.

71.4% of the book's participants have received a high school diploma. (One participant was not asked this question).

100% of the book's executive/media participants do not have tattoos, do not smoke, have received a high school diploma, and are undecided as to who to vote for in the 2012 U.S. Presidential Election.

TALES FROM THE STAGE

TABLE OF CONTENTS

Bruce with Grand Funk Railroad at the Sound Board in Detroit,
March 2012. Photo by Craig Clingan

Bruce Kulick

Lead Guitar

Past-Meat Loaf, Blackjack, Billy Squier, Kiss

Present-Grand Funk Railroad, ESP

MT: When is your birthday?
BK: December 12, 1953.

MT: The city you were raised in?
BK: Brooklyn, New York.

MT: The city you currently reside?
BK: Los Angeles, California.

MT: Marital status?
BK: Divorced. Currently in a relationship.

MT: Any children?
BK: No.

MT: Did you graduate high school? What year?
BK: Yes. 1973.

MT: How old were you when you picked up your first guitar?
BK: I was about 10. Right after I saw the Beatles.

MT: What type of musical training did you receive growing up?
BK: At first I had picked up some stuff from my brother, Bob (Kulick). Then there was a record shop that had a guitar instructor down the block in Brooklyn. I took some lessons from him. And then later on I went to Queens College, and took some music courses, but I also took some private instructional courses from a jazz musician to help learn theory and expand my guitar awareness.

MT: Your first big break occurred in 1977 when you toured with Meat Loaf supporting *Bat out of Hell*, along with your brother, Bob. What do you recall from the tour?

BK: It was huge! He went from nothing to a superstar, so it was really eye opening for me. In some ways it was quite stressful, but it was an amazing experience for sure.

MT: How were you treated by Meat Loaf?

BK: You know, he was going through some ups and downs, and I kind of hid from any of the drama. My brother kind of went knee deep into it, and I just watched from afar. (laughs).

MT: Do you and Meat Loaf still communicate?

BK: Yes. I run into him on occasion, and he did Rock 'n' Roll Fantasy Camp one time in which I interviewed him for the campers, which was fun.

MT: Following your experience in Meat Loaf, you started the band Blackjack with a then unknown, Michael Bolton. How did you two meet?

BK: He was popular on the east coast, and my brother knew him. My brother knew that Michael was looking to do some live shows, and needed a guitarist. I was then introduced to him through my brother.

MT: Deep down, is Michael Bolton a 'Rocker'?

BK: He definitely can rock. Yes!

MT: You did two albums with Blackjack then went in the studio to record "Tale of the Tape", the debut from Billy Squier in 1980. How did you get hooked up with Billy?

BK: My brother had done some demos with him previously, and Bob wasn't available when Billy went into the studio. Billy heard that I was available, so he asked me to do it.

MT: What was the reason you didn't stay in the band for his next album, *Don't Say No*?

BK: That was a tough one. I really wanted to tour with him and continue on, but Blackjack had a supposed commitment from our record company at the time to do more. I was loyal to Bolton and Blackjack. Then he (Billy) went on to be huge, but quite honestly if I would have stayed with Billy, I probably wouldn't have gotten the Kiss gig.

MT: Did you have any resentment in 1981-1982 when Billy's hits were all over the radio?
BK: It was hard for me. No doubt. But when a door closes another one opens. I always kept the bigger picture in mind, but it was pretty weird to just see him totally explode. (laughs).

MT: In 1984 you landed one of the most sought after gigs in music playing lead guitar for Kiss. How did they find you?
BK: I knew them from years prior. Not very well, but I hung out with Paul a little bit as Bob had worked with them. So socially, I knew them a bit. But what it really came down to was people talking about me, and they needed some help on the *Animalize* record. Maybe something had happened to Mark St. John right then, I'm not sure, but I got a message from Paul. Once I spoke with him and wound up doing some guitar work for Kiss on the *Animalize* record that Paul was producing, he said, "Don't cut your hair." That basically meant, "If we need somebody, we're calling you."

MT: How long did you have to learn the songs Kiss was playing on tour?
BK: What was interesting is that I had injured my arm prior to going into rehearsals, so that made it pretty scary. But I was still able to listen to the songs. I think that I only had a month to prepare. We had four weeks of rehearsal planned, but I think I only caught the last 10 days of rehearsal because my arm had to heal. It was a little scary.

MT: Was there a particular song that you had trouble learning?
BK: Mark was a little more of a speed metal, flashy-type player, so some of his riffs were kind of like, "huh?" But none of the vintage stuff. It was just a few of the tracks on *Animalize*, like, I think it was "In to the Fire." I was just like, "Oh, boy," but I made it my own, I made it work, and I made it exciting too. But, I wasn't that comfortable with it.

MT: You joined the band on the Animalize tour, but it was Mark St. John who played on the album. Did you ever get to meet Mark?
BK: Well, actually Mark and I traveled together for a while when they were trying to see if he really did deserve the job. So we were on tour, and Mark was traveling with us, watching and learning. I kept it very peaceful, and we would jam backstage a little bit. Then they tested him out on the first half of the show, then the second half of the show, then a full show. And then they sent him home.

MT: Early on, were your nerves worse playing live with Meat Loaf or Kiss?
BK: Oh, definitely Kiss. You have to remember with Meat Loaf there were nine people on stage, so it wasn't that big a deal.

MT: Being that you were so young in Meat Loaf, I thought that the rush would be similar?
BK: Yeah, but with only four guys on stage, and the pressure of being the Lead Guitarist for Kiss. My knees were trembling during the first gig.

MT: Between 1984 and 1996, you did five studio albums with Kiss. Do you have a favorite?
BK: I would have to say *Revenge* is my favorite, but there were highlights on all of them. But I thought that *Revenge* was the best of what we were capable of.

Bruce on the Revenge Tour with Kiss in 1992. Photo by Nicola Coccarone.

MT: How did the writing process work with Kiss?
BK: Most of the time, Paul was writing with people like Desmond (Child) as they had some great success prior to me joining the band. Hopefully, I was always able to tease them with a riff or two and try to get in there. So, I did co-write with Desmond and Paul, which was wonderful. And sometimes, Adam Mitchell and Paul. Gene's approach was different in that he would write a million things, throw them against the wall and see what sticks. The hardest part for me was trying to figure out who would like a particular riff, because if one of them passed, it was kind of spoiled. So, it was a little tricky but my instincts were always pretty good as to what to do. They viewed me as a great guitarist, but I don't think they viewed me enough as the song writer that I think that I am. But, I wasn't going to step on their toes.

MT: Can you talk about how the publishing was split?
BK: I don't have an issue talking about the publishing. They didn't give publishing until the very last album, *Carnival of Souls*, which was interesting. It was split for what you contributed. We discussed who should get what, and it actually went rather smooth. The downside was that for the other albums I didn't receive any publishing. But, I understood that. When you walk into a big corporation, you don't get shares right away. You have to earn them.

MT: Is there a song or two in particular that you felt you should have received a bigger share of the publishing on?
BK: Not really. "I Walk Alone" was interesting. Gene really wrote all of the lyrics, and he had the melody, and he wrote some of the music. So he was more of the writer than me, and I think we split it 60/40. But at the time, since I spent so much time on the song demo-ing it and making it work, I thought it would be a 50/50. But in the end when I looked at what he really contributed, I couldn't argue. So, no, I really didn't have a beef about that kind of stuff. Even if I wrote the music, I didn't write the lyrics, I didn't write the melody. Believe me, in my position it was just wonderful to have a "co-write" at that point in my career.

MT: There were many highs as well as somber periods during your time with Kiss. When you joined the band Eric Carr was Kiss's drummer. What was Eric like?
BK: It was interesting. Here is Eric as our drummer, which is a much envied position. We were touring England, and he was just miserable. I was yelling at him, because let's face it - here I am, not really having a gig in New York. Now I'm touring the world with Kiss in a limo, and flying first class. I was kind of upset with him. But, you need to live a day in their shoes, and see what they're doing, and see why they are so upset and I started to understand Eric's frustrations. Although I always thought he could have handled it better, because you need to look at the big picture with those types of gigs.

MT: Eric was diagnosed with heart cancer in March of 1991. How did you learn that he had heart cancer?
BK: The first time he called me about it, he said he had a tumor on his heart. They didn't know how severe it might be. Obviously, when they eventually did the surgery is when they found out it was cancerous. I remember I was in The Cineramadome movie theatre calling him from a pay phone. As he was telling me about his tumor, I was staring off

into space thinking about the severity of open-heart surgery, and what they might find. He wasn't feeling well after the holiday, or post tour into spring. And that's when he learned he was really sick.

MT: Rumor has it that during the peak of his treatment for the disease, he pleaded with Paul and Gene to let him appear in the video, God Gave Rock n Roll to You. What do you remember about Eric and making that video?
BK: I remember that he picked me up from the airport in his rental car. He had a nice Kiss wig on, that didn't look any different than his real hair, and he played his heart out. He had more energy than I did. I couldn't believe it, but it meant a lot to him. You can see in his face in the video and photos that it's kind of drawn. You can tell that he wasn't healthy and fighting a disease, but I must say that he was very brave.

MT: Eric Carr passed away in November 1991 at the age of 41. What are your fondest memories of him?
BK: Eric was wonderful with the fans, and an incredibly talented musician. The size of his abilities weren't always shown in Kiss, not everyone's does when you're in a big machine-sized band, you know? The guy was really incredibly sweet, and incredibly talented. He loved his fans, and they knew it. He was the one guy who was most accessible. Back in the day when there was literal fan mail, he would write back to everybody, and even call some of them! I remember once in Sweden. It was 10-degrees outside, and the hotel wouldn't let the fans come into the hotel lobby. Eric went out in the freezing cold and signed autographs for the fans. That's the kind of guy he was.

MT: After Eric Carr's passing, Eric Singer became Kiss's drummer. Then in 1992 the Kiss album, *Revenge,* was released. Is it true that ex-Kiss guitarist Vinnie Vincent was called on to assist in the writing of that album? How did that make you feel?
BK: I'm not sure that he was called on, but at some point he must have realized that they (Kiss) are still going on, and doing well, and maybe I can write another song with them. I won't say anything about Vinnie personally, but he is a talented guy. So the next thing I know he was working with Gene and (Bob) Ezrin, or Paul and Ezrin on some song ideas. As much as there was a part of me that was a little jealous, Vinnie had written a lot of stuff on the *Lick It Up* album. I don't know what he did to piss them off back then, contractually or otherwise, but Mark St. John became their new guitar player overnight. But here was a guy who had a real ability and knowledge to write with those guys, so

18

he was reintroduced to the situation and they welcomed it. The egos were checked at the door for *Revenge*, and that's why it is such a great record.

MT: In 1995, Kiss appeared on MTV's Unplugged where for the first time in years original members Peter Criss and Ace Frehley played a few songs with the band. Speculation ran rampant about a reunion tour. How was the news officially broken to you regarding the Reunion Tour?

BK: The news of the actual Reunion Tour wasn't really broken to Eric and I until months later in January. We were called up to a meeting at Gene's guest house. By then all of their ducks were in a row. I thought it was very brave of them, and probably very smart of them to continue recording *Carnival of Souls* and having Eric and I in the band. I guess while all of these negotiations were going on, those guys (Ace and Peter) are wild cards. Who knows what could have happened? Why blow up a working situation - even though it's not as profitable? That version of Kiss was still a very functional band. The good part about it, even though I was crushed and always knew that it could happen, was that they kept me on salary for a full year and I didn't do anything. Eric as well. I don't even know what the contract read. It could have only required two weeks pay, but they went beyond that. It was nice of them to do that.

MT: Have you ever hung out with Ace?

BK: Not really one on one. I haven't really "hung out" with him. We have always said respectful things about each other, but I am the guy who replaced him, you know? I don't think he's the kind of guy who is going to just chill. But he knows that I have always been aware of his status within the band, and have shown respect towards it.

MT: How is your relationship with Gene and Paul?

BK: It's great. I was recently at Gene's wedding. He appeared on my solo record, "BK3". I just attended Paul's 60th Birthday party. Only his close friends were invited, so I am honored that we are still all close. I am still part of the family. I didn't expect that to go away, but I know that they don't have to do that. I have a very healthy relationship with those guys.

MT: While in Kiss, who was considered your boss?

BK: Well, really Gene and Paul *were* my boss. I know when I would reference it that way, they didn't like it, but it was true. They made the decisions. Of course, there were always business people around them, but even when they had a manager that I was very good friends with, they still made the decisions. It was pretty obvious. Sometimes they would play Good Cop/Bad Cop. I could go to Gene complaining about something, and he would say, "Have you talked to Paul?" (laughs). I didn't complain much to Paul about Gene. Gene is Gene, you know? But if there was something that I couldn't get through to Paul on, I would ask Gene. And Gene would say, "You need to talk with Paul."

MT: Did you have anything in your contract that prohibited you from doing anything dangerous?
BK: I don't remember if there was a clause in there, but I think they knew that I wasn't that type of person. I remember when Paul went skiing. I asked him, "What are you doing?" I mean, what would happen if he broke something?

MT: What were your favorite Kiss songs to play live?
BK: Most of the stuff from *Revenge* was a lot of fun. I really liked some of the classics. "Detroit". Obviously, "Rock N Roll" you could get played out on. Any of the songs like "Crazy Nights" from my era I loved playing. I liked when we got a little deeper and did "100,000 Years", "Watchin' You", "She". We didn't always do those songs, but I enjoyed playing them. Those are great songs, and with Eric and I playing them, they were maybe a little more super-charged live.

MT: How crazy were the after parties with Kiss?
BK: Because you're in a big band, there were always girls around. No one was doing drugs. I mean, Eric Carr would drink a little bit. But, we always had a good time if we wanted to go out, and sometimes that was as simple as bowling parties. At that stage of the band, we were not acting insane like Guns N' Roses from that time.

MT: After Kiss, you hooked up with John Corabi and formed Union. How did you hook up with John?
BK: I was very close with Larry Mazer, who managed Kiss for a while when I was in the band. I really trusted Larry, and he suggested that I do something with John. He told me that John was no longer working with Motley Crue, and he thought that the musical chemistry with us would be good, and he was right. John and I are both very different people personality wise, but it worked.

MT: Your next project was Kiss drummer, Eric Singer, the Eric Singer Project (ESP) along with John Corabi. That band seems like a ton of fun.
BK: It is! Because of our schedules, it is hard to plan far in advance for our gigs. We have never done an original song, and just play covers. Sometimes a Union song, a Kiss tune, maybe Alice Cooper. We play songs from bands that we like, or bands that we have been in.
Although we have put out a live DVD from Sydney, we have never taken it too seriously. It has been a fun side project for all of us, and we do enjoy it when we have the time. But the scheduling for it has been brutal with everyone being in different bands

Touring with ESP. Pisa, Italy, 2011. Photo by Andrea Tessieri

MT: In 2001 you released your debut solo album, *Audio Dog*, then *Trasformer,*and most recently, *BK3*, your third solo album, which is amazing. Do you have a favorite?
BK: *BK3* is my favorite. There are songs on "Audio Dog" and "Transformer" that I am very fond of. But the vision of what I could be, and working with Jeremy Rubolino who is such a great Producer, I feel I gave my best to *BK3*. Obviously I had some amazing guests on that record. It was an evolution, and now that I have set the bar with *BK3*, my level of commitment will have to be the same moving forward.

MT: You also joined your current band in 2001, Grand Funk Railroad (GFR). How did you hook up with them?
BK: I had met Don Brewer, GFR's drummer years ago at a NAMM show, and we had visited several times since. Actually I knew him from a tour that I had done with Michael Bolton years ago, when Michael was opening for Bob Seger. Don plays drums for Bob when he tours. I just think that I was on the short list. I know that they wanted a real strong guitarist. We had emailed a few times, spoke on the phone, and then he flew me to Michigan. It's hard to believe that this is the eleventh year that I have been in the band.

MT: Can we expect any new studio stuff from GFR?
BK: That is up to Don and Mel, and for whatever reason, they are not very ambitious about it. We do some new songs live, but the answer is unknown to me because I am not in control of that. (laughs).

MT: Your website, www.kulick.net, is incredibly up-to-date, and is very comprehensive. Who provides the consistent updates?
BK: Fortunately, I have met some amazing people throughout my years in Kiss. Chris and Beth White have been friends and fans of mine for a long time, and happen to be Tech Whizzes! They have been part of Team Kulick for years now, and do an amazing job updating everything for me. I am glad that they are there for me, and I am always grateful of their support.

MT: Answers.com estimates your net worth to be between $14-15 million. Is that accurate?
BK: (laughs) I saw that, too. Very pathetically, no! (laughs).

MT: Do you own any stocks?
BK: I have a pension that is managed by a Portfolio Manager. I realized I don't want to be in that game, and he is doing well with it. I don't know from day to day where the pension is being invested.

MT: If you were asked to do MTV's Cribs, would you do it?
BK: No.

MT: How large is your current home?
BK: I have a lovely townhome that is about 2000 square feet.

MT: What vehicles do you own?
BK: I love Lexus! I have two Lexus's.

MT: Are you registered to vote? Will you be voting in November (2012)? Who for?
BK: I am registered, I will vote, and I am a Democrat.

MT: If it were a simple process, would you have any of your tattoos removed?
BK: I don't have one! (laughs).

MT: Who is the best vocalist you have ever played with?
BK: Wow (long pause). You know, I'm just going to say it. Not a lot of people know him, but the guy I am working with now in Grand Funk (Max Carl) is the most consistent, best vocalist I have worked with.

MT: Do you smoke cigarettes?
BK: No.

MT: What was your drug of choice back in the day?
BK: I smoked pot.

MT: If you took a drug test today, what would it tell us?
BK: That I drink a lot of water. (laughs).

MT: Do you not drink alcohol at all?
BK: I have an occasional glass of wine. I am pretty boring as a Rock Star! (laughs).

MT: Should marijuana be legalized?
BK: Yes.

MT: Craziest Groupie story?
BK: Well, this goes back awhile before my Meat Loaf days, around Madison, Wisconsin. I remember these two women picking me up at a bar. I go to their beautiful townhouse, they were making out in front of me, and I can't wait to see what happens. This was like Penthouse Letters for me! They had taken Quaaludes which were very popular back then. This one that I *really* liked started not feeling so well, and got sick. I wasn't real unhappy with what was left, because she was still really hot. But, I was envisioning the threesome and it didn't happen.

MT: But you still did ok?
BK: Yes, I still got laid! (laughs). No doubt about it. Again, it wasn't from the girl that I really wanted, but this other girl was still awesome.

It's just that my fantasy went right down the tubes once the really hot one got sick. Apparently that drug can make you throw up.

MT: When you were on tour with Kiss, how much did you get for your food per diem each day?
BK: They solved that problem really easy. We just signed for whatever we wanted.

MT: And GFR?
BK: We are on our own. But we're fed, and have food at the hotels Happy Hour, so it's not a big deal at all.

MT: When is the last time you paid for or changed your own guitar strings?
BK: I changed my strings for Fantasy Camp last week. I don't pay for strings. I will admit that.

MT: Who are the three best rock guitarists that are living today?
BK: I really like Joe Bonamassa now. He's a sweet guy as well. I think that Joe Satriani is still amazing. And I saw a video of Eddie Van Halen playing live recently, and he was amazing.

MT: Is there a band that you have toured with who you did not get along with?
BK: Well, I wasn't touring with them at the time, and now I am friends with them, but I was backstage at a Cheap Trick show and a security guard threw me down. (laughs). It fucked up my toe. He didn't realize that it was okay that I was back there. But there was a gig in Canada - Kiss and Whitesnake. I didn't have anything against them, but apparently David Coverdale was threatening to steal Gene's wig. It was one of those crazy things. Word was getting around. It just made us play better to be honest with you.

MT: Who are you listening to these days?
BK: I like the new Coldplay stuff. I have to get the new McCartney record. I have already heard it, and will be listening to that. I don't immerse myself with a whole lot of metal stuff, but I did hear the new Slash song and I really dug that. I will be getting that record as well.

MT: What is the most eccentric thing on your rider?
BK: We don't get too crazy with Grand Funk. At one point, we had Foie Gras (duck liver) on our rider. I didn't put it on there, Mel did. I

looked at him one night and said, "You have to be kidding me?" (laughs). For me, it's like, "Can I please have some Club Soda?" I have never been a real Rider Nut. Even in Kiss, it was always simple foods. Nothing exotic. Then I would go see Van Halen, go back stage and there would be fuckin' lobster and steak everywhere! (laughs). In Kiss, we would just have roasted turkey and tuna fish. The Kiss riders were never extreme. Lavish, but never extreme.

MT: What was the first expensive item you bought from your first big pay day?
BK: A Lexus. And then I started buying nicer guitars. I remember thinking, "I can actually buy the guitar in the window now."

MT: Should Kiss be in The Rock and Roll Hall of Fame?
BK: Absolutely!

MT: When was the last time you were blown away by a band's live performance?
BK: I watched the Foo Fighters on the Grammy's. They kicked total ass! They are a great band.

MT: What band mate of yours is (was) constantly late for lobby call or sound check?
BK: Oh, yes. Most of the time, Paul was.

MT: The best rock album ever produced?
BK: *Abbey Road* by the Beatles, with Producer George Martin.

MT: What is your current role with Rock 'n' Roll Fantasy Camp?
BK: I am one of the go-to Counselors, as I have had a lot of experience with the camp. It's an amazing experience. Not only are the campers blown away by its intensity, but it is an incredibly rewarding experience for me as well. We take people from all different talent levels, record something that is respectable, and kick some ass on stage too!

MT: Who are you endorsed by?
BK: ESP Guitars, Seymour Duncan pickups, and SIT Strings. I have great relationships with people at Gibson and other companies, but I don't go chasing them down.

MT: When is the last time you paid for a guitar?
BK: Oh, most of the time, except for what ESP provides me. And even then I buy ESP's on eBay. If there is a model they don't make anymore, how can they help me? I just bought two white Vipers with gold hardware late last year. What did I play at Fantasy Camp last week? Those. What did I play in Australia last month? One of those guitars. Just last week I bought a J-185 Gibson from one of my favorite local guitar shops. It is such a great hobby, and there is a song in every guitar the way I look at it.

MT: What advice would you provide someone who wants to play rock music for a living?
BK: For someone to feel that they are just going to make a living at playing music is foolish. You need to love it, and enjoy it. Be ambitious with it, and be the best that you can be. Have an original take on what you are trying to do, and be realistic. The music business is a very hard one, but don't ever lose the love of the music.

MT: What are you working on now? How can people get a hold of you?
BK: As you mentioned, my website is wonderful, www.kulick.net. There's merchandise on the website, and I have an email address on there in which I try to personally answer most emails. I have a personal page on Facebook which I have maxed at five thousand friends, but I also have the Official Bruce Kulick Fan Page in which I can add an infinite amount of friends or fans. I post the same thing on each, so nobody will miss out on anything. I have just started writing new songs for the next BK solo record. I am hoping to do more of the Rock 'n' Roll Fantasy Camps. I continue to stay busy touring with Grand Funk. I am hoping to do some more Europe travel, and head Down Under again. And maybe get over to Japan later in the year. Some people are talking to me about that. Each day is different. You never know what email you're going to get, or what phone call you're going to get.

Jay with Malice at the Long Beach Arena, 1986.
Photo by Nigel Skeet.

Jay Reynolds

Lead Guitar

Past-Megadeth

Present-Malice, Metal Church

MT: Do you have a nickname?
JR: Not really. People call me a lot of things.

MT: Date of Birth?
JR: October 16, 1959.

MT: The city you were raised in?
JR: Houston, Texas and Portland, Oregon.

MT: The city you currently reside?
JR: Portland, Oregon.

MT: Did you graduate from High School?
JR: Yes, in 1978.

MT: Do you rent or own the place you call home?
JR: Right now, I rent.

MT: How big is it, and how much is your rent?
JR: It's like $800. It's a large one bedroom. It's not the opulence that I owned in the 80s. It's a little over 1,000 square feet.

MT: Is your current home the biggest you have ever owned?
JR: Absolutely not. The nicest place I owned was a two bedroom, two bath condo in Redondo Beach in the 80s. I should have never sold it. It's probably worth a couple million bucks today.

MT: What is your relationship status?
JR: I have a girlfriend of two and a half years. She plays guitar in a band as well.

MT: How old is she?
JR: 23.

MT: When did you pick up your first guitar?
JR: I started taking acoustic guitar lessons when I was about 10 years old. They really didn't teach me what I wanted to learn, so at 13 I traded my acoustic for a bag of weed. Then when I was 14 or 15, I saw a guitar in a pawn shop. It was a Gibson Melody Maker. I think it was $80. I bought it and never looked back.

MT: Do you remember the first time you thought you were good enough to make a living playing guitar?
JR: Yeah. I was in my bedroom getting ready for school blasting some UFO. I looked at myself in the mirror and noticed that my hair was becoming really long. I was also becoming an accomplished guitar player, devoting more time to playing guitar than schoolwork. I had a flash thinking that I could do that too. I remember that day like yesterday. I must have been about 17 at the time.

MT: Brian Slagel with Metal Blade Records put two songs on the first *Metal Massacre* album featuring Malice, in which you were a founding member in 1982. Malice shared the album with a then unknown Metallica and Ratt, as well as others. How did Malice get to that point so quickly?
JR: That is a long, but good story. I moved from Portland to Southern California with my drummer buddy, Mike. We moved with the sole intention of starting an all original band, so the nucleus of Malice started around 1980. We were auditioning people, and found it difficult to find players that had the whole package. So I ended up calling all of my friends in Oregon who played in all of the best heavy metal bands that I knew before, and I had talked Mick Zane in to moving to California with us. So now we had three guys down here. During this time, I was actually writing for Brian Slagel's fanzine called "The New Heavy Metal Revue." This was before he had Metal Blade. Brian was a good friend and worked at a record store, Oz Records. He furnished me with all of my import metal albums. This is when Brian started to put the album together, and I told him, "I have a band." At the time I didn't, but Mick and I flew to Portland and immediately jumped in the studio with three other guys we knew to record two songs. The next day, I rented out a concert hall and we did a photo session. I had a lot of money at the time. We then sent out our photos and demo around the world. We actually had the cover of Aardschok (metal magazine from

Holland) before we were even a band! The two songs on Metal Massacre came out before we even had the bands full lineup. We were getting gig requests, radio airplay, and press coverage before the band became a band! I then had enough ammo to entice the three guys from Portland to move to LA. Our original drummer, Mike, moved on. We did our first live gig together Thanksgiving night in 1982, and Metallica opened for us.

MT: Malice's second album, *License to Kill*, received more commercial success than any other Malice album. You toured with WASP supporting the album. What was that like?
JR: Well, it must have been good, because Blackie called me a couple years later to audition for W.A.S.P. We actually toured with many bands during that time - Nazareth, Alice Cooper, Armored Saint. We were on the road a lot.

MT: Who was the craziest guy in W.A.S.P.?
JR: Obviously, Chris Holmes.

MT: Any good stories?
JR: Oh, of course, dude. Chris is still a good friend. I saw him just last week. One night after both bands played the Troubadour, we rented rooms at this fleabag hotel on Sunset. It's no longer there, but was called the Beverly Sunset. It was Chris's birthday party. This is how he used to drink. He had a half gallon of vodka. He poured about an eighth of it into a glass, then put a little bit of orange juice into the half gallon of vodka. That was his cocktail! I drank from the glass he poured the couple shots into, but Chris polished off his half gallon of vodka in an hour! (laughs). That turned into an insane night.

MT: Later that year, Malice went to Europe opening for Slayer. This pairing was a self-admitted mismatch musically. Were you worried for your safety while on stage over there?
JR: We actually saw people killed on that tour. I don't think we were ever worried for our safety. We were all ten foot tall and bulletproof in the 80s. We had no fear, but we did get spit on in England and Scotland!

MT: Is it possible to defend yourselves on stage from being spit on?
JR: We came up with a routine in which we would all pee in a big bucket prior to the show. We had gone out and bought a bunch of squirt

guns. The roadies would fill up the squirt guns with piss, and if anyone spit on us too much we would get out the piss guns and nail them!

MT: Malice was featured in the movie "Vice Versa" with Judge Reinhold and Fred Savage. How did the movie appearance affect the bands popularity?
JR: Well, we got a lot of notoriety from it. Basically the movie came out as the band was breaking up. We shot that scene a year before the movie came out.

MT: Were there drugs on the movie set?
JR: In the 80s there were drugs everywhere, but not on that movie set. Our shoot took two days, but they put us up for five nights in a five-star hotel in Chicago, with limos on call. We took over one of the radio stations and had parties at the Limelight every night.

MT: Why do you think that Malice never received a high level of commercial success?
JR: Our initial first album was released much later than it should have been, and bad management.

Malice at The Roxy in Hollywood, 1985.
Photo by Lisa Lea

MT: Do you still receive any sort of income or publishing monies from Malice?

JR: Yes, we still get checks to this day. We have music on TV and movies, and that typically pays well. We get quarterly checks from BMI that used to be in the thousands of dollars, but are now $5 to $500.

MT: What happened to Malice's original vocalist, James Neal? Do you two still talk?

JR: Yes, I just emailed him recently. In 2007 when we reformed Malice, I asked him if he wanted to do it, and he declined. He felt there was too much 'bad blood' under the bridge. We had a little falling out with him over the alcoholism. We made him sign a contract to not drink on the last tour, but he still did sometime.

MT: Dave Mustaine from Megadeth writes about you in his biography, "Mustaine, A Heavy Metal Memoir." He mentions how in 1987 you briefly joined Megadeth, but in the studio you called on the assistance of your guitar teacher, Jeff Young, to play your parts. Is that how it went down?

JR: Not exactly. David Ellefson and I are good friends, and I basically moved into the Megadeth camp for two weeks auditioning after we came off the "License to Kill" tour. Before I had moved in with the Megadeth guys, I had lived with a whole bunch of roommates in this massive house in Hollywood, including Jeff Young. He was going to GIT, and he would help me at times with my guitar playing, but I wouldn't really call him my guitar "teacher." So the Megadeth guys tell me I have the gig with them replacing Chris Poland. Obviously my work load was big learning all of their stuff, so I asked Jeff to help me with Chris Poland's leads. This way I wouldn't have to take the time learning them by ear, note for note. When we entered the studio and it came time for my leads, I did tell them that my guy was going to come in and assist me to write some really cool stuff. It wasn't like I wanted him to play my parts for me, but I wanted to create the best solos that I could create. At that point, everyone was so high that there is no real right or wrong version of the story. I am still friends with Dave and David, and I actually lived with them for another month after I was fired. But I did have a lot to do with that album. I was the one that suggested we do "Anarchy in the UK" and getting Dave to a vocal coach. Junior (Ellefson) was the glue that held the band together and we made a good team, but it was the 'good ole - bad ole' days for Megadeth and everyone was doing a lot of drugs at the time.

MT: Mustaine also mentioned that you were a "well-connected drug user." Is that a fair assessment?
JR: Yes. At the time I was.

MT: If you took a drug test today, what would it tell us?
JR: Actually, I am clean now. I drink a little beer, but that's it.

MT: How much would you guess you have spent on drugs over the years?
JR: It has to be over a million bucks, but the cost is difficult to calculate. If you consider the trips to rehab, all of the money you could have made, and so on. I have been to rehab a couple times and have had a couple relapses, but I'm too old for that shit now.

MT: How is your health?
JR: I am in really, really good health for my age. I don't look my age, I don't act my age, and I don't want to.

MT: Lastly, did Mustaine forewarn you about mentioning you in his book?
JR: No, but it was no surprise at all.

MT: Years later you joined Metal Church. How was the experience different than being in Malice?
JR: Metal Church was a much bigger band. We spent a lot of time in Europe. We toured constantly, and made some really good records. I was really fortunate to get that opportunity as it got my name back out there, and I plan on being fully involved with them again either next year, or the following when we come off of hiatus.

MT: Which gig paid better?
JR: I made a pretty decent salary in Metal Church especially towards the end when we had some momentum going when everything fell apart. (laughs). I was making over $2,000 a week on some of the tours, plus all of our expenses.

MT: Did you participate in the writing process with Metal Church?
JR: Yes, I did. I wrote on each album. I didn't have a lot of input, as Kurdt has written almost every Metal Church song from day one, but Kurdt does allow a co-writing process. I received some publishing, and have no complaints.

MT: What was your favorite song to play live with Metal Church?
JR: Oh, all of the stuff off of the first album "Beyond the Black," "Metal Church," "Battalions." The second album was killer as well. The newer stuff was fun too, but the old stuff would send chills up your spine playing to a live festival crowd of 40,000 -60,000 people, you know?

MT: When you lived in LA in the 1980s, where did you typically hang out?
JR: Hollywood and the beach. We all loved The Rainbow.

Jay at the Keep It True Festival with Malice, April 2011. Photo by Henk Bosma.

MT: How much of your current income is music related?
JR: 20-30%. Sometimes more, sometimes less.

MT: What do you do outside of music to make ends meet?
JR: I am a sales manager that sells Direct TV, Dish Network, phone and internet service which I have been doing for about ten years. It's a great job that allows me a lot of flexibility to tour, record, and make good money.

MT: How do instrument endorsement deals work?
JR: If you have an album on a larger label coming out, and you're going to be touring, you can get some stuff for free. At NAMM, I just renewed my endorsement with ESP. Alan Steelgrave with ESP has always taken great care of me. Since Malice will be touring again soon, they give me two or three guitars with cases a year as long as I am touring. I also secured a couple new deals as well.

MT: Do you follow the stock market?
JR: I used to. I used to have sizable investments, but my retirement plan isn't what it used to be.

MT: When is the last time you set an alarm to wake up to?
JR: Yesterday.

MT: What was the first expensive item you bought from your first big payday?
JR: The coolest thing I ever bought was that condo in Redondo Beach. It was only $150,000 at the time, but I know it's worth millions now. I should have never sold it, but when we moved to New York, I thought I would just keep making money, but oh well!

MT: What kind of car do you drive now?
JR: I actually drive a Volkswagen.

MT: Do you have a favorite car that you have owned?
JR: I have owned Corvettes and Porsches that I liked.

MT: Do you follow politics? If so, who will you vote for in 2012?
JR: I do, but I try not to. It's such a mind fuck that I try to stay out of it now. I am registered to vote, but I'm undecided right now as to who I will vote for.

MT: If it were a simple process, would you have any of your tattoos removed?
JR: Since I never have gotten a tattoo, no!

MT: You have never gotten a tat?
JR: No! I was going to get sleeves, and I never got around to it. I love tats, I just never did it.

MT: What makes you laugh?
JR: Anything and everything. I don't take anything that seriously.

MT: Who is the best musician that you have ever jammed with?
JR: There are a few, but I'll say drummer Deen Castronovo, and Slash.

MT: Do you smoke cigarettes? How many a day?
JR: Yes, about a half pack to a pack a day.

MT: If you could write your own ticket, and play lead guitar in any band, who would you want to play for?
JR: Motorhead, hands down!

MT: Tell us about your worst groupie experience?
JR: (laughs). Waking up in a hotel room in North Carolina in a pool of blood! And looking over with a bad hangover going, "Oh my god, did I do that?"

MT: Did you typically wear protection?
JR: Sometimes yes, sometimes no.

MT: How many times have you had sex in your backstage dressing room?
JR: I couldn't count. Hundreds of times, maybe.

MT: If you had to guess, how many women have you been with?
JR: I don't know. You put all the tours together, and obviously I have been in monogamous relationships as well, so I don't know. Hundreds and hundreds. I just can't remember all of the names and faces. After thirty years of playing Rock 'n Roll, it's a blur.

MT: When you're on tour, how much do you get for your food per diem each day?
JR: Usually around $35.

MT: When is the last time you paid for/changed your own guitar strings?
JR: I haven't bought guitar strings in years, but I change my own quite frequently.

MT: What band are you listening to in your car right now?
JR: Ratt! I just ran into Warren DeMartini the other day. He just played some shows out here with Uli Roth.

MT: Who are the three best guitar players in metal today?
JR: Yngwie, Uli Roth, and Michael Schenker.

MT: Have you ever gotten into a fist fight with a band mate?
JR: Not a band mate, but a sound guy! I had to throw down on a sound man during a Metal Church tour. (laughs). We were playing the Crocodile Rock in Allentown. After the show this sound man was talking shit about me behind my back, so I just fucking called him on it. He got in my face, so I had to put him down.

MT: Who is the one person in rock'n'roll that you run into knowing you're going to have a long night of partying ahead of you?

JR: Man, there is a bunch of those guys. I've had a couple drinkathons with the Slayer guys. And Alexi (Laiho, Children of Bodom) is always up for getting hammered. I just recently drank with him at the NAMM show. I run the other way when I see a lot of these guys coming because I don't do the drugs anymore (laughs).

MT: Tells us about the last time you got sick before or during a show.

JR: Back in the Malice days, I remember being awake for a couple days at a time. I wouldn't get high before a show, but sometimes I was so exhausted that they just about had to prop me up in front of my amp. But the adrenaline kicks in, the crowd is there, you sweat it out, and you're ready to party after the show.

MT: When was the last time you were blown away by a band's live performance?

JR: I see a lot of live bands, but it's been a while since I have really been blown away. Probably when I saw Arch Enemy at Wacken in 2006. They kicked our ass all over the stage, and I just didn't expect that from them. I thought that was pretty cool.

MT: What is the best rock album ever produced?

JR: *Appetite for Destruction* from Guns N' Roses, or if you want old school, *Heaven and Hell* from Black Sabbath.

MT: What advice would you provide a guitarist looking to play rock music for a living?

JR: Don't give up your day job, dude! (laughs). Learn the other aspects of the industry. You need to have great chops, but you have to know how to write songs, you have to learn the business, maintain your appearance, and create album concepts. There is so much that goes into making it. The kids now have such a huge head start with the internet. We never had that.

MT: We understand Malice is back in the studio. When can we expect to hear the new stuff?

JR: The new album will be out in May 2012, and we will be touring in May 2012. We'll be in Europe by June 2012, and we'll take it as far as we can. Then we'll be back in the studio doing another album by year's end.

MT: How can people get a hold of you?
JR: I'm easy to find on the internet. Just Facebook me. I would like to see Metal Church get back together, quickly. So that's my priority. Malice now, Metal Church down the road.

Herman at sound check with Michael Schenker in Tokyo, Japan.
March 2012. Photo by Michael Voss.

Herman Rarebell

Drums

Past-The Scorpions

Present-Herman Ze German & Band, RAREBELL

MT: Do you have a nickname?
HR: Herman Ze German.

MT: When is your birthday?
HR: November 18, 1949.

MT: The city you were raised in?
HR: Saarbruecken. It's in West Germany.

MT: The city you currently reside?
HR: Brighton, England.

MT: Did you graduate high school?
HR: Yes, in 1968.

MT: Marital Status?
HR: I am married to Claudia Raab Rarebell.

MT: Any kids?
HR: My daughter, Leah, is from a previous marriage. She will be 23 in August (2012).

MT: Tell us about your first experience with the drums while at a wedding when you were thirteen?
HR: Well, after the wedding was over and everyone was drunk, I sat behind the drum kit and began playing around. I noticed immediately how fun it was to play the drums, and I also noticed that I had a good feeling for rhythm.

MT: You excelled at playing drums, and began playing in bands while in school. At the age of seventeen you realized that you could make decent money playing music. What gig did you land?

HR: In Germany, I didn't go to what they call high school. I went to a school of Economics, which is basically equal to College or University in America. It concentrated just on Economics. My dad wanted me to become a businessman, you know? So I was seventeen years old playing in a school band called, "The Mastermen." Funny name for a jam band, huh? (laughs). But after that, I found myself in my first professional band called, "Fuggs Blues." With this band we played the American air bases. We made really good money for that time, so I quit school and told my mother and father that I was going to become a professional musician.

MT: How did you feel about your father asking you to go to music school in your late teens?

HR: Yes, he asked me to go to the Music Academy in Saarbruechen. I told him that I would go if that made him feel more secure about my future. I went to the Music Academy and spent about two and a half years there, you know? But while I was there, I learned that my heart was really in to rock music. So I told my dad this, and also told him that I was going to move to England. I was going to try to make my luck there, as well as try to find a band there. My dad drove me and my drum kit all the way to Oostende, which is in Belgium. We caught a boat there. I loaded my drums on to the boat, and everything was shipped to Victoria Station in London. In the beginning, I had friends in London so I could stay with them while I was getting adjusted to England, but my dream did not come true. I did not find the next big heavy metal band. I really dreamt in Germany that I could join Uriah Heep, or another Led Zeppelin, or another Black Sabbath, but nobody was waiting for me there, of course. After four to six weeks my money was gone, so I worked as a gardener or barman. But then suddenly, some people realized that I could read music. So, I became a highly requested session drummer in London, as I could work in the studio very fast. Then one day, I met another German musician there by the name of Michael Schenker.

MT: You received your first big break in early 1977 when your friend, Michael Schenker, informed you that his brother, Rudolf, needed a drummer for his band, the Scorpions. What did your audition consists of?

HR: We all met a few nights before, and Michael introduced me to Rudolf. We got along immediately. Rudolf told me that he would audition me in a few days at a place called The Sound Circles in London. I thought I would just be auditioning by myself, but when I showed up there were 50 or 60 drummers there! I thought, "Oh shit, they didn't tell me this!" (laughs). I played the audition. We played two or three songs, but I can't remember exactly what songs they were. After the audition I got the usual, "Don't call us, we'll call you." So I packed up my drums and left the building. I said to myself, "They're never going to call you, so continue with your life." I would go back being a session musician, and make my living that way. Sure enough, the next day I get a phone call from them. They told me that they liked me very much, as well as my drumming, and asked me if I would like to join the band. If I said yes, they wanted to take my drum kit back with them to Hanover. They also had a plane ticket for me that I could use during the next week. I told them that I had to talk to my girlfriend, and could not leave that night, but they could take the drums if they wanted. That's what they did. They took the drum kit to Hanover, and a week later I was also in Hanover.

MT: Some fans may not realize that you were an incredibly active songwriter with the Scorpions. Where do you think you got this talent?
HR: I think it's because when I joined the band, I spoke the best English. Obviously, I had lived in England from 1971 to 1977. During the recording of my first album with the Scorpions, *Taken by Force*, Rudolf took a liking to, "He's a Woman, She's a Man." That was the first song I wrote the lyrics for in the band.

MT: When you joined the band, Uli Roth played lead guitar for the Scorpions. Although he toured in support of *Taken by Force*, Uli was not happy with the commercial direction that the band was headed, correct?
HR: He wasn't happy at all. One of the first things I said to Rudolf and Klaus when I met them was that I saw their gig at the Marquee Club. I noticed they had two directions in the band. You had Uli's direction, which was very Jimi Hendrix influenced. Then they had the other direction which was melodic rock, which was Rudolf's and Klaus's direction, similar to Uriah Heep. In talking with Rudolf, I said, "If you really want to be successful, you have to make up your mind which direction you want to go." Rudolf, Klaus, and I took this position. After we toured Japan, and after we did the *Tokyo Tapes* album, Uli

announced he would not be with us on the next album, and would be leaving the band. If you take a look at some of the lyrics on *Taken by Force*, for example, "I've Got to Be Free," you can see that he wanted to do his own thing.

MT: You auditioned nearly 140 guitar players looking for Uli's replacement, and hired Matthias Jabs. During this time while you were touring in 1978-79, the Scorpions shared a bill often with AC/DC. How well did you know Bon Scott?
HR: I knew him very well. After the shows we would usually go out together, if we were staying in the town that we played. We would go to the local clubs, and jam with the local bands. It was awesome. We toured and opened for AC/DC, Aerosmith, and Ted Nugent, and then they added a special guest to play before us. A band from England named Def Leppard.

MT: Did you ever hang out with fellow drummer, Rick Allen, from Def Leppard?
HR: Oh yeah. We used to smuggle him into the clubs because he was only 16 or 17 at the time. Cliff, the drummer from Ted Nugent, and I used to tell the doormen at the clubs, "Don't worry, he is with us. He just forgot his passport, but he is 21." (laughs). In those days all of the bands that were signed to our management, Leber-Krebs, became friends and knew each other. Especially when you are on the road together for months and months and months. You get to know each other backstage, you're of the same age group, and of course you want to party after the show.

MT: Shortly after Jabs joined the Scorpions, Michael Schenker returned to the band after reportedly being kicked out of UFO for his excessive drinking. Is that what happened?
HR: No, he didn't get kicked out of UFO, he left. I think he had a big fight with Phil Mogg. After the fight, he came back to Germany. He wasn't actually ready to rejoin the band. He was just kind of there, you know? He played on several songs on *Lovedrive*, including the first guitar solo on "Loving You Sunday Morning."

MT: At that time, how did your drinking compare with Michael's?
HR: Well, I think that we were both drinking huge amounts of alcohol at that time. Let's put it this way. Michael had his own drinking habits that didn't compare to mine. He could drink in the morning, which I never did, you know? I usually drank after five or six in the afternoon.

At the time, it was just how it was. You would go in the studio and before you would start playing you would have a few beers, then start recording.

MT: Months later, Jabs was let go, giving Michael the lead guitar spot once again. It's well documented that Michael's drinking created problems, including unexpectedly not showing up to gigs. How was this handled?
HR: Well, I spoke to Rudolf about it. I said, "Look, Rudolf. You need to talk to your brother. He has to be reliable; otherwise, we cannot go on." Because one day he would show up. The next day he wouldn't show up. So, when Michael didn't show up for one of the shows, we asked Matthias to come back, and he did. After the show, Matthias said, "Look, I have helped you out for the last time. But I won't help you again. You need to make up your mind regarding who you want, as you cannot count on me anymore." So, I said to Rudolf, "Matthias is right. You can't fuckabout with a guy like this. He is a great guitar player. I know that Michael is your brother, but we need to make up our minds." We really didn't know if Michael even wanted to be in the Scorpions at the time, and as we all know he started MSG (Michael Schenker Group) just a few months later.

MT: Jabs was named as the permanent lead guitarist for the Scorpions again in April 1979. In 1980, the Scorpions released the album, *Animal Magnetism*, which included the hit, "The Zoo." The bad news was that Klaus Meine was experiencing throat pain. Did you realize how serious his throat problems were?
HR: Klaus started experiencing bad throat pain when we started recording *Blackout*. I remember when we went to the south of France to record *Blackout,* the band got together and Klaus told us that his throat problems were so big, that he suggested that we get another singer. He didn't think he would recover. We told Klaus that we were not only musicians for our business, but that we were all close friends, and we would wait for him to recover. He informed us that could take a year. We said, "Ok, then we'll wait a year for you." And that is what we did. We waited for him until he was ready to record again.

MT: While Klaus was recovering, you started working on the album, *Blackout.* Is it true that Don Dokken's voice was used in the studio to hit some of the high notes on this album?
HR: No. To clear the air on this, Dieter Dierks found Don Dokken in a club in Hamburg, and thought he was really good. All Don did was

sing some guide tracks for us, so we knew where the vocals would be while recording. He did not invent the vocal line. Klaus had already established that. So to this day, Don is just a very good friend. As you know, he sang three songs on my solo album. He helped us out when Klaus was ill, but we never considered him to be the singer in the band, and he knew that. He was just a friend helping out.

MT: So, Don Dokken's voice is not on *Blackout* at all?
HR: Don Dokken is not on *Blackout* at all.

MT: As with other Scorpions albums, you were given writing credit for more than half of the songs on the album, including the title track, *Blackout*. What was the story behind the lyrics to that song?
HR: We played one night in Dubuque, Iowa. We had played with Judas Priest, and Def Leppard. After the show, we went back to the hotel which was a Best Western. Rudolf got really drunk that night, and he came into the hotel lobby where everyone was watching TV. He took a full can of beer off of the table, and poured it into the back of the TV. The TV started smoking just like in the movies! (laughs). So, I took him to the elevator and got him up to his room. Then the next morning I asked him, "Do you remember what you did last night?" (laughs). He just looked at me and said, "No." And I said, "You had a blackout." I started to write lyrics that morning in the hotel, and a few days later he came up with the riff. So we had the song, "Blackout", and later on we said, "Why don't we call the album, *Blackout*?" That was my suggestion, and I'm happy that the band took my suggestion.

MT: Was it around this time that you recorded your first solo album, *Nip in the Bud*, which was re-released as *Herman Ze German and Friends*?
HR: Absolutely! As you can imagine, during the time that Klaus was recovering I had more than nine months to twiddle my thumbs. Being a very active person, I decided to release my solo album. I had written many songs with two partners of mine, D.H. Cooper and Pedro Schemm. We rehearsed in my hometown of Saarbruechen, and we also recorded there, and the result was *Nip in the Bud*. A year later, I went to Los Angeles. Everyone was telling me that it was a great album, and singers were coming up to me wanting to be on the album. Don (Dokken) said that he could sing a few songs better than what we had originally recorded. Then Jack Russell came into the studio and wanted to sing a song. Then Bobby Blotzer and Juan Croucier from Ratt

wanted to be involved. Charlie Huhn from Ted Nugent sang a song. And I'm proud to say that the famous Steve Marriott from Small Faces also sang a song on the album called, "Having a Good Time."

MT: Klaus fully recovered after throat surgery, and *Blackout* was released which is now Platinum. The band's success landed them a slot at Day 2 of the US Festival in 1983 in front of nearly 400,000 people. The Scorpions performed with Motley Crue, Quiet Riot, Ozzy Osbourne, Judas Priest, Van Halen, and others. How cool was that gig?
HR: I think that was the coolest gig we had done in America at the time. I believe, until this day, that it was that gig that made the band big in America. The message went all over the country, not just California, and everybody in America suddenly started to talk about the Scorpions.

MT: Do you remember what you were paid to perform at the US Festival?
HR: To be honest with you, I do not remember. I really don't.

MT: What was the backstage scene like?
HR: It was unbelievable. You have to think about this. You had to be flown in by helicopter, as it was not possible to reach the venue by car. Nobody expected so many people to attend the festival, and the roads were completely blocked. So, our tour manager suggested we rent a helicopter and fly in, which is what we did. So the backstage area was actually quite big with lots of trailers from all of the bands playing that day.

MT: Were all of the bands partying backstage?
HR: Not on this day. There was no party time after we played. When our gig was over we had to be flown immediately out of there, as there would be no other chance to get out with all of the traffic.

MT: The Scorpions appearance at the US Festival catapulted the bands popularity to a new level. Then in 1984 *Love at First Sting* was released. You wrote the lyrics for the mega-hit, "Rock You Like a Hurricane." What was your inspiration?
HR: The inspiration was being on the road, you know? When you listen to the first lines, "It's early morning and the sun comes out. Last night was shaking and pretty loud. My cat is purring and scratches my skin, so what is wrong with another sin?" Do I have to tell you anything more?! I'll tell you what happened. At five in the morning I

opened up the curtains. I had partied the whole night, and the sun had just come up. I was sitting down at a desk, and I literally wrote those lyrics in a half hour because the inspiration was there. My cat was still in bed purring! (laughs).

Herman in Athens, Greece. July 2009.
Photo courtesy of the Greek Scorpions Fan Club

MT: As with some of the previous "racy" Scorpions album cover art, you were forced to change the albums cover art in the US. How frustrating was this for the band?
HR: Well look, when you come from Europe seeing a tit is not a big deal. We see them every day during the summer on our beaches, as long as I can remember. So, years prior when we did the *Lovedrive* album, we had chewing gum put on the tit of a woman on the album cover. The cover was designed by a company called, Hipgnosis. As you know, they did the covers for many of the Pink Floyd albums. When they showed us the cover for *Lovedrive*, we all thought it was a fantastic cover, and we wanted to run with it. So when the American record company saw this, they had to put it in a red vinyl to hide most of the cover art. But because of this, everybody bought it! (laughs).

Playboy voted it album cover of the year, and the album went gold immediately.

MT: Dieter Dierks had produced every Scorpions album since you joined the band, including *Love at First Sting*. How did you like working with Dieter?
HR: Dieter and I have a very, very close friendship to this day. I wish the band would have taken Dieter back after the band had the experiences with Bruce Fairbairn, and Keith Olsen. I think that Dieter is 'thee' Scorpions' producer. He made the sound that made the Scorpions.

MT: You toured extensively supporting *Love at First Sting*, which went double platinum a few months after its release. You were living the dream. What were the backstage parties like on that tour?
HR: I think that those were the best backstage parties ever! Don't forget, this was the mid 80s. There was no AIDS. There were no huge problems in the world as there are now. It was really just a party-party-party 24 hours a day.

MT: Did you have a particular party buddy in the band at that time?
HR: I partied a lot with Matthias, I partied a lot with Rudolf, I partied a lot with Francis. Klaus was always watching his voice since the operation. He was not able to drink anymore, indulge in any excesses or go without sleep. He never did any drugs. I think he learned his lesson before we did the *Blackout* album.

MT: One of your opening acts on that tour was Bon Jovi. What were they like to tour with back then?
HR: At the time they were managed by Doc McGhee. Doc told the guys in Bon Jovi, "Stand on the side of the stage, and watch what the Scorpions do when they're on stage. Copy that, and I promise you that you will be a very successful band." And as we all know a year later in 1985, the new Bon Jovi album was produced by Bruce Fairbairn, and he had his first big album in America, *Slippery When Wet*. So they watched us really good! I'll tell you something funny. A few months ago, Bon Jovi played in Munich, Germany and he played "Rock You Like a Hurricane" on stage. None of us were there to hear it live, but I heard that he said very nice things about us at the concert in Munich. He said that we influenced him, and that we were always very nice to

him. When we toured with them we always gave them enough space on stage to perform properly. We gave them the full sound, and the full lights, so there was really nothing they could have complained about. Until this day I have a friendship with those boys, and when I see them it's just like going back in time to those good ole days.

MT: Along with the success of the album came the need to cater to the MTV crowd. The band released four videos from *Love at First Sting*. Do you enjoy making videos?
HR: Personally, I do. In those days it was a perfect outlet for us to reach everybody in America. When you had a new song, you could just present it on MTV. These days MTV doesn't play any rock videos. It doesn't matter if it's AC/DC or Aerosmith, MTV doesn't play rock music anymore.

MT: The Scorpions released two more successful albums in the late 80s, and then in 1990 the band played at the Roger Waters performance of *The Wall* in Berlin. What was that like?
HR: It was fantastic! Remember, I grew up in West Germany, and all of my relatives were in East Germany. That meant that you could not go and visit them as there was a wall separating you. Now, suddenly you are playing in Berlin, in the middle of 'nowhereland' where the wall was previously. As I was on stage there, I have to admit that I had tears running down my face as I looked out at 380,000 people watching us as the band that opened the show that night. I remember we opened with "In the Flesh."

MT: Did you get to play "Winds of Change" that night?
HR: No, all of the songs were from *The Wall*. But "Winds of Change" was already running on MTV at the time. It was being played on the radio stations in Germany, Russia, and America and became a huge hit for us. The song was basically the soundtrack for freedom in the east. Suddenly, this freedom spread all over the East. It went from Russia to Hungry to Eastern Germany. Nobody could hold back the young people any longer. Everybody wanted to go to the west, and they wanted to be free.

MT: Shortly after that performance the bands long time bassist, Francis Bucholz left the band. Rumors circulated that he was caught embezzling from the band. Can you shine some light on why he left the Scorpions?

HR: To go into the whole story would require the rest of the evening. (laughs). We had fights like any other band. The outcome from this particular fight was that we all said to Francis, "We think it is better if you go." He agreed with us, and he left the band. A little after Francis left the band, I was then producing an album for D.H. Cooper, and needed a bass player. Ralph Rieckermann came highly recommended to me. I flew him to my house in the south of France to record, and he played very well in the studio. So, I phoned Klaus, Rudolf, and Matthias and told them that I think I found our new bass player. A few days later, Ralph and I both flew to Hanover. We went in the rehearsal room, and a few hours later he was the new bass player in the band.

MT: The Scorpions released, *Face the Heat*, in 1993, and *Live Bites* in 1995. Did you know that your time with the Scorpions was nearing the end?

HR: Yes, I did. In the early 90s when grunge came into the mix, I knew that the era of melodic rock was over. At least that's what I thought at the time. So I thought, "Now is the time to do something else, because this isn't going to go on forever. Maybe you should start producing, or do something all together different." Then in 1995 after *Live Bites* was released, the album that followed was *Pure Instinct*. I didn't write any of the songs on that album, and I no longer agreed with the bands direction. For my taste, it was too soft.

MT: Late in 1995, you left the Scorpions. How was the band informed of your departure?

HR: In December of 1995, I met with Klaus, Rudolf, and Matthias. I told them, "I have an offer to start a record company in Monte Carlo. We're going to call it Monaco Records. I want to do something else." They said, "Oh no. You can't do this. Don't go. You can't leave us after 20 years." I said, "Look, everything comes to an end. This is the end for me. The music scene has completely changed, and I don't like the direction that you want to go in. I don't want to play soft rock. I want to start my record company and do something completely different."

MT: You then started your record label with an influential friend of yours.

HR: I lived in Monaco then moved to Monte Carlo in 1985. Over the years, I became friends with Prince Albert. He is a drummer as well. From our friendship came the idea to start a record company, as there was no record company in Monaco at the time. When the direction of the band changed, and I was completely out of the writing situation - I wasn't even asked anymore to help write the songs - I figured it was the right time for a change.

MT: Jumping way ahead to 2006, you played on stage with the Scorpions at Wacken. Michael Schenker and Uli Roth also made guest appearances with the band. How did it feel to play with your friends again?

HR: It felt great! Absolutely great! I also played with them in 2010 at a festival in Oklahoma. It always feels good to see them and play with them. Remember, we have a very long friendship. I still visit with them when I can. Matthias has a guitar shop in Munich, so when I am in Munich I go visit him, and we'll have dinner. It's the same with Rudolf. But, I know that the whole thing is done. I believe that we have done a great job with the band. I was the first one to leave, but now that band has made a decision to call it a day. They are on their Farewell Tour right now.

MT: You have played with three of the best guitar players in the world. Who do you feel is the best of the three?

HR: That is a very good question, and it is very hard for me to answer. They all have their qualities. Actually, it's impossible to answer. How can you compare an Uli Roth with a Michael Schenker, and then Michael Schenker with Matthias? When it comes to playing Hendrix songs, there is no one better than Uli. When it comes to playing beautiful melodies, no one can beat Michael. When it comes to putting everything together, Matthias is amazing. It's too hard to say. They are all equally good.

MT: Lately you have been active promoting your most recent solo album, _Take It As It Comes_. What was the inspiration behind the album?

HR: I am a guy who always likes to try new things. I got tired of the hard rock schedule, which I did for so, so long. So, I said to my wife Claudia, "Let's do something different." As you know, she is a killer sax player, she looks fantastic, and we are a very good team together. That was the inspiration behind the album.

MT: Also, you have a new book out, "And Speaking of Scorpions." Did you enjoy the book writing process?

HR: Yes, I enjoyed it very much. In January 2011, my co-writer, Michael Krikorian, visited me in Brighton. He spent 10 days there with me interviewing me and going over all of the facts. I told him my whole life…basically what I am telling you now. He put it into wonderful words, and I am really, really happy with the outcome of this book.

Sound check with MSG, Glasgow Scotland. July 2011.
Photo by Billy Hepburn/MusicPro (UK)

MT: How excited are you to tour playing for Michael Schenker this year?
HR: I am very excited! I played with Michael last summer in England when we were the special guest for the Black Country Communion tour. We also played the High Voltage Festival 2011 in London in front of 35,000 people. If you go to YouTube, you can see us play, "Rock You Like A Hurricane," as well as see me sing from that show. That was probably our best gig on that tour. Michael played better than ever, and maybe the best he has ever played. He has not taken any drugs in the last two years, nor has he had any alcohol in the last two years. He is totally clean, and he is playing better than I have ever heard him play.

MT: How do you feel the last night of a long tour? Are you happy or sad?
HR: Both, you know? I usually have one laughing eye and one crying eye! (laughs). One part of you thinks that it is good to have some time off, maybe have a holiday or relax. The other part of you is thinking that it's sad that the tour is over. Every artist lives off of the applause

from the audience. There is no better feeling in the world than when you perform and the audience appreciates what you do.

MT: What kind of car(s) do you own?
HR: I have a Mercedes and a Jaguar.

MT: Are you in a financial position to never have to work again?
HR: Yes, I am. I wrote about 35 songs for the Scorpions, and "Rock You Like a Hurricane" alone is played every day on about 150 radio stations worldwide. It's a highly requested song for advertisements. Currently it's in the movie, "Killer Elite." Last year it was in a Budweiser advertisement, and now Microsoft wants to use it. The requests are endless to use the song.

MT: Speaking of your songwriting, is it true that you have 78 Gold, and 30 Platinum records to your credit?
HR: Yes, I do. Don't forget, the Scorpions alone have sold 100 million CDs over the years.

MT: Do you smoke cigarettes?
HR: I don't smoke at all. Occasionally, I will have a glass of wine with dinner. My bad drinking habits stopped 10 years ago, when I got married.

MT: What was your drug of choice back in the day?
HR: I would smoke marijuana.

MT: If you took a drug test today, what would it tell us?
HR: I would pass it, and be considered one of the healthiest people at my age. I am totally healthy, and my wife looks after me very well. Being a drummer, I need to be fit. Don't forget, I am going to be playing in front of thousands of people in Japan in a few days. You cannot do this at my age if you are going to do drugs, and drink alcohol.

MT: Craziest groupie story?
HR: Where do I start? (laughs). You know, there were so many mornings that I woke up and said, "How did you get here? What is your name?" It's really hard to say. Don't forget one thing. In the 80s, life on the road was a consistent party. I must have had a different girl every night.

MT: How many women would you guess you have been with?
HR: Well, how many dates did I play? (laughs). Look at the period that I was in the band…count all of the dates we played. That's how many women I have been with.

MT: Is there a band that you have toured with who you did not get along with?
HR: Not really. I'm a very friendly human being. I even got along with Ritchie Blackmore and Ted Nugent. How many people can say that?

MT: Should the Scorpions be in The Rock and Roll Hall of Fame?
HR: Absolutely!

MT: What advice would you provide to a drummer who wants to play rock music for a living?
HR: If you really believe that you are good, practice, practice, practice. And believe in yourself. Believing in yourself is the key to everything.

MT: What are you working on now? How can people get a hold of you?
HR: People can get a hold of me through my website, www.hermanrarebell.com. My direct email address is info@hermanrarebell.com. If you want to ask me a question, this is the email address to send it to. I am currently promoting my book, "And Speaking of Scorpions." I am currently talking with publishers in Brazil, France, Germany, Russia, and Japan. My goal is to release this book in every language on the planet.

Ripper with Iced Earth in 2007. Photo by Henk Bosma.

Tim "Ripper" Owens

Lead Vocals

Past: Judas Priest, Iced Earth, Winter's Bane

Present: Solo, Beyond Fear, Charred Walls of the Damned, Hail!, Dio Disciples, Yngwie Malmsteen

MT: Your birthday?
TO: September 13, 1967.

MT: The city you were raised in?
TO: Akron, Ohio.

MT: The city you currently reside?
TO: Akron, Ohio.

MT: Marital Status?
TO: Married

MT: Any Kids?
TO: I have 3 kids, a granddaughter, and another grandchild on the way.

MT: Did you graduate high school?
TO: Yes. In 1985.

MT: Were you active in Choir type groups in High School?
TO: Oh, yes. That's what got me through. I was part of all of them. Select Choir, Madrigals, Glee Club. I was in every music program that I could possibly be in to keep me out of math and science.

MT: Were you one of the more popular kids in high school?
TO: I was alright. I had a sense of humor. I was nerdy. I was a metal head, but I was still nerdy. I was bigger, kind of the chubby guy as I was 230 pounds. I was the one bringing Judas Priest records into Choir.

MT: When was the first time you knew your voice was something special?
TO: As a little kid I would always sing. Elvis, Kiss, whatever. I'm not sure when it was, but I knew that I could always sing. I think the wide range came from singing in my earlier bands, but I realized that I could sing anything, any style. Whether it was Choir singing, or Slayer; I could sing it all.

MT: Like many musicians, your first bands were cover bands. Who were some of your favorite bands to cover?
TO: Obviously Judas Priest, but Metallica, Metal Church, Anthrax, and Savatage. So, they were a little bit different than most.

MT: Being such a huge fan, how bummed were you when Rob Halford left Judas Priest in 1992?
TO: I was pretty bummed, but I liked the *Fight* record that he put out, and thought that was pretty cool. I was a fan of Priest and a fan of Rob's, and for me, I was excited that Rob had put out the solo record. It did bum me out a bit, as he left right after *Painkiller* which was one of their best albums in a long time.

MT: Your first original band, Winter's Bane, gigged frequently around Akron. What did you like most about that band?
TO: Well, actually my first band was called Brainicide. It was some of the best stuff that I have ever done. It was crazy music, and really out there. But Winter's Bane was a great thing. We went to Germany and recorded a record with Massacre Records. It was a really bad time for heavy metal. This was in the early 90s and heavy metal was at one of its lowest points.

MT: Is it true that to capitalize on revenue and bookings, that the members of Winter's Bane formed a Judas Priest tribute band, "British Steel", that would appear on the same bill?
TO: Yes, that is exactly what we would do. We were trying to book Winter's Bane with no luck. So this agent, Greg St. Charles from Long Distance Entertainment, suggested that we form a Judas Priest tribute band. Judas Priest wasn't together at the time, and he suggested we open up as Winter's Bane, and then come back out as the Judas Priest tribute band. That's what we did. It was probably the downfall of Winter's Bane, as it probably hurt that band, and eventually broke it up, but that's what we would do. That's true.

MT: Do you recall what the band was making for shows like that?
TO: It was all over the place. Probably between $500 to $2,000 at the most.

MT: What did you do to make ends meet back in the day?
TO: Well, I always worked. I worked at a law firm for about six years. I started as a file clerk, and ended up as a purchasing agent. Then I when I was trying to do a little more in music, I became a salesmen. I sold printing, and that allowed me to travel more.

MT: After "British Steel" disbanded in 1995, you were fronting an alternative rock cover band, "Seattle." Were you fed up on heavy metal at that point?
TO: No, I left the Judas Priest tribute band because the band didn't sound that good. I didn't sound good, my voice wasn't the same, everything was bad and I couldn't do it anymore. The "Seattle" tribute band was just there and I wanted to do it. Vocally, it actually took as much out of me. Singing the high notes of Chris Cornell is just as hard as anybody.

MT: Enter Christa Lentine and Julie Vitto. What was your relationship with them?
TO: They were fans and lived in Rochester, New York. They had come out to the "British Steel" show when we were there. They were friends of Scott Travis, the drummer for Judas Priest. They made it out to one of our last shows in Erie, Pennsylvania and videotaped the show. They were great.

MT: So take us back to that day in February 1996. The phone call.
TO: I happened to go by my parent's house. While I was there the phone rang, my mom answered it, and said "It's for you." I picked up the phone and it was Julie. She said, "We have been trying to find your number. We couldn't find it anywhere. All that was listed was your parents' number. But, Judas Priest wants to talk with you. Scott called me and asked me if I had your info. I told him 'no', but he asked me if I could find it. You need to call Jane Andrews with Judas Priest, here's the number!" So at the time, all of my stuff, including my old albums, were at my parents house. I went upstairs and found the Judas Priest album, *Painkiller,* and looked for her name. There it was! "Jane Andrews." I was like, "Wow! This is really Judas Priest!" So, I called and she said, "We want to audition you. You probably aren't going to have to sing, we have heard the video tape. We just want to meet you.

Do you have a passport?" I said, "Yeah." She asked me, "How soon can you be on a plane to England?" I said, "Whenever". She had to confirm times with everyone, so she called me back a while later. This was on a Saturday. When she called me back, she asked if I could leave Monday. Of course, I told her that I could. So after a night with no sleep, I am finally able to fall asleep Sunday night, and the phone rings at 10 pm. It was Scott Travis from Judas Priest. "Hey Tim, this is Scott. Listen, the band is here and we're watching this video tape. Everything sounds so bad on this thing except your voice. So we want to make sure that you weren't dubbing your vocals in, because it sounds too good." I was amazed, because here is the band calling me! But I assured them that it was really me on the tape. I was on a plane the next day, and that was it.

MT: Monday morning you flew to England to audition for Judas Priest. What were your nerves like walking into the studio to audition?
TO: It was pretty crazy. Jane picked me up at the airport, and I was driven to Wales - which was hours away, to a studio that Black Sabbath recorded at. When I got out of the car, I could hear guitar playing and drumming. I'm like, "Oh my god. This is Judas Priest in there playing!" The thing was, I didn't think that I was going to have to sing. I didn't even practice singing. I hadn't sung a Judas Priest song in over a year, and I wasn't ready to sing. We walked into the kitchen, and there is Ian Hill sitting eating breakfast. I was like, "Wow!" So she took me in and there is Glenn playing guitar and Scott playing drums. It was crazy. I was nervous, obviously. I mean these were guys that I grew up idolizing, but they made me feel comfortable right from the start.

MT: What song(s) did you sing for your audition?
TO: Here's what they said: "Let's get dinner tonight. Get some sleep. Tomorrow we're going to sing." I'm like, "Uh oh, what?" They confirmed that they wanted me to audition tomorrow. I didn't say anything, but I'm thinking in my head that they told me that I wasn't going to have to sing, and I wasn't prepared. I looked at them and said, "You know what? I would rather just do it now, because I won't be able to sleep tonight." Even though I was going on no sleep, and knew that this wasn't going to be my best singing, I might as well just get it over with. They were ok with it, so I went up and showered. When I came back down they put on "Victim of Changes." They used an old live version, and took Rob's vocals out. They were in a control room,

and I started singing the song. I sang the very first line of "Victim of Changes", and Glenn said, "Alright Owens, you've got the gig!"

MT: Once you learned that you had the gig, was compensation discussed? How did you know what you would be paid?
TO: They did it right away. They put me on a retainer. At that time I thought it was great, you know? Judas Priest always treated me well, and I have a good friendship with them. They paid me to record, and I got paid more to do tours. It's funny because I make much more money now in my career than I ever have. Most people would think the opposite. But, I'm also much busier now than I ever have been.

MT: It's well known that the movie "Rock Star" was loosely based on your career. How accurately was this portrayed in the movie?
TO: Not accurate at all. The idea for the movie "Rock Star" came from a huge article in The New York Times, which was an unusual thing for them to feature a hard rocker. I'm not sure what it was called, something along the lines of, "Unleash the Ripper," but they came to my hometown, there were pictures of my parents, it was this big giant thing. So, George Clooney's company bought the rights to it. It was going to be called "Metal Gods" and the movie was more of a story about me than the band. I think that was a little upsetting. Even though it was the story of Judas Priest, the story was really my story. But there were a lot of similarities in what they were doing that the band didn't like, like focusing that they were an aging band. But then they started adding things that weren't accurate. So, the band asked for some sort of creative control with the movie. They told us that we could have zero input, and the band said, "We want nothing to do with the movie." So when that happened, they had to change a lot of things in the movie, so that they wouldn't have to pay us.

MT: Did they pay you at all for your story?
TO: They paid me nothing. I made zero. They just based it loosely around the news article.

MT: What did you think when you heard that Mark Wahlberg would be playing you?
TO: That's the only time in my life that I've had abs! I'm a fan of his, and I thought it was pretty awesome. The funny thing is that it was offered to Brad Pitt originally, given his relationship with George Clooney.

MT: Back to JP, what were your nerves like for your first Judas Priest gig?
TO: First of all, our shows were much smaller than the shows in the movie. (laughs). We weren't playing arenas. My first gig with them was at a place called The Boathouse in Virginia Beach. I wasn't super nervous because I was ready. We were prepared as a band, and I was prepared as a singer. That stuff was made for me to sing. I didn't have to change my style and try to imitate, I was just singing like myself. I remember when I walked on stage there were some chants of "Ripper," and it made me feel at ease right away.

MT: With Rob Halford being the "Metal God" himself, he obviously had a huge loyal following. Do you recall specific instances of disrespect aimed at you during live performances?
TO: You know, I really didn't experience that anywhere. Actually, that happened in New Orleans. Every time I played there, there were a couple guys with long blonde hair and mustaches, wearing old denim jackets, stuck in the 80s. They would stand about three people back from the stage, and just flip me off the entire show. It's funny as I remember talking to Ronnie Dio about this, and Ronnie was like, "Man, I used to get that all the time in Black Sabbath." Ronnie and I had experienced a lot of similar things that we would talk about. But, the best part about the story is the last time that I was in New Orleans, we were doing "Diamonds and Rust." I was singing it my own way, and hitting these high notes. I would always try to get the crowd to sing, and these guys flipped me off for years. Finally, they just put their hands down and started singing, "Diamonds and Rust." It was like I had finally won these two guys over.

MT: You remembered these two dudes, all of these years?
TO: These guys would stand in the exact same spot at the House of Blues in New Orleans. What's funny is that these guys bought tickets, went there, stood in the same spot, and flipped me off! Finally, they started singing, "Diamonds and Rust," and it was like I won. They probably still hated me, but they were like, "Alright, we give." But the fans were always good to me. I know that they wanted Rob back. I understand why they wanted Rob back, but I just wanted the fans to *listen* to me sing the songs. Listen. Enjoy it. But the fans were always great to me. They were awesome.

MT: Did it take some pressure off of you when your first studio album with Judas Priest, *Jugulator*, was nominated for a Grammy?

TO: That was awesome! I never had pressure, but I always knew that people wanted Rob back. Whatever I did, wasn't going to please some people. If Rob Halford would have been nominated for that Grammy it would have been the best thing in the world, or if Rob Halford would have recorded *Jugulator* it would have been the best record ever, but because I did it, it's looked at a little differently. But, that was a big moment. That was something that no one could take away from me. People often leave that off of my resume when they say, "Tim'Ripper'Owens, who sang for Judas Priest." How about, "Grammy nominated, Tim "Ripper" Owens?" That's a pretty awesome thing.

MT: In sports, players receive bonuses for being MVP or being awarded the Golden Glove. Did you receive a bonus for your Grammy nomination?
TO: No. I got to go to the Grammy's, so I guess that was kind of a bonus. That was pretty awesome.

MT: You appeared on two live albums with Judas Priest and two studio albums. Do you have a favorite? Why?
TO: I like *Live in London* a lot. The DVD especially. It's wonderfully shot. The backstage stuff, the sound…I think it's one of the best DVDs that I have ever seen. I like it a lot because there are no overdubs

vocally. We flew from Japan to that gig, and I was beat. My energy was a little bit down on stage, there were flat notes, I messed lines up, but it's *me*. And it still sounded pretty good, and it was not fixed. As a studio record, I like both of them. They are both different. I like songs off of each record, so I don't know that I could narrow it down.

MT: How did the writing process work with Judas Priest?
TO: Glenn was the main guy. I would come in, they would have some lyrics, and we would piece it together. They were the hardest records that I have ever done, because I would have to go over it and over it, and over it again, and we would write it as we were doing it. They would always tell me, "Just to make sure you know, this is the same way that we did it with Rob." We would record all day long. It was a long, long tedious process.

MT: Did you receive publishing on the albums you did with Judas Priest?
TO: No, no. I always wanted to give them my input, and they were always like, "Next record you can." I cut them some slack on that because it was Judas Priest. I wasn't going to argue with them, I was happy to be in the band. Jumping ahead, when I joined Beyond Fear I wrote the song, "Scream Machine." It's a very Judas Priest-like song, and it is one of the most well-received songs that I have ever done in my career. It's about a metal machine, which is a very Judas Priest-like thing. It was kind of like saying, "Judas Priest could have had me write with them." That song could have been on any Judas Priest record.

MT: In 2003, you learned that Rob Halford was returning to Judas Priest. How were you informed?
TO: I was informed by an email from Jane. I had just recorded the *Iced Earth* record, because there was nothing going on. There was no money coming in and it was just a bad time in my career. You could see the end coming. I told my wife that I wished that Judas Priest would fire me, because I would have never quit. But there was so much more to do, and I couldn't do it because I was handcuffed. I needed to make more money. So, about a week later we were leaving town and I checked my email before we left. I read the email from Jane and it said that they were going bring Rob back. You know, even though it was an email, I wasn't upset at how it was handled. I ended up talking with the guys. It was handled very professionally. They compensated me, and everything was handled very well.

MT: You had joined the band, Iced Earth, and did several albums with the band before they brought back their original vocalist. Did you feel jinxed?

TO: No! Here's the funny thing about that. Judas Priest was a good fit for me. Iced Earth wasn't a good fit. I felt like I wasn't respected by a few people with them. I wanted out of the band, and I was trying to figure out how to do that, but I think he may have known that. That one wasn't handled well. I was let go a week before Christmas, by an email, as I was on the way to his house. There was no compensation, and I was just thrown to the wolves. It was an unfortunate situation, and handled very poorly. It was a good run, great records, good concerts. I had good times with them, but it ended on a sour note. But, I landed on my feet and started working right away, so I didn't feel jinxed. Iced Earth just wasn't a good fit for me.

MT: During your time with Iced Earth, you had also started a side project, Beyond Fear. How often do you gig with this band?

TO: I don't too much now, but I did then. We put the album out, and did a bunch of world tours. When I left Iced Earth, I had to figure out how to make a living. That's when the solo record came about, and now I tour a lot solo. 75% of my touring is solo, under "Tim 'Ripper' Owens." People want Beyond Fear, but financially it's a harder thing to do.

MT: In 2008, you joined forces with Yngwie Malmsteen. How did you two hook up?

TO: Yngwie had actually called me before I left Iced Earth. Four days after Iced Earth, I was in Miami talking with Yngwie. I thought that it would be fun to make a record with him, and that working with him would be an opportunity to make some new fans, and have people see me who have never seen me before. Iced Earth fans were similar to Judas Priest fans, but Yngwie fans were different. So, I thought, "Let's try this." It's Yngwie Malmsteen. He one of the top guitar players in the history of music!

MT: He has a reputation for being difficult. Have you seen that side of him?

TO: I get along great with Yngwie. I had a great experience with him recording the album, and when I tour with him it is a great time as well. I do my thing, he does his. He respects my singing and brags about me all of the time. Really, I get along with him. I get along with the whole band. It's a good time.

MT: In 2009, you released your solo album, *Play My Game*. Can we expect more solo stuff?
TO: I would like to do it. I had so many guests on that album. Michael Wilton, Tony Franklin, Billy Sheehan, Rudy Sarzo, Doug Aldrich. Everybody is on there, but I would do it differently next time. I would like to do a solo record, and just use the guys in Dio Disciples for it. It's just so hard right now with my scheduling. Right now I would like to re-record my solo record, re-release it with some bonus footage because SPV filed for bankruptcy right after I recorded it. They owe me a lot of money. They didn't put the album out there for people to buy. So I would like to redo it and put it back out there.

MT: Also in 2009, you started "Charred Walls of the Damned" with Richard Christy. What are the future plans for that band.
TO: That is probably one of the best received things that I have done. It's on Metal Blade. That's Richard's baby, but Richard is busy on the Howard Stern show and there is not a lot of time to tour. I think that when I join a band, everyone knows that it's going to be hard for me to do a lot of touring anyway, so that works out. We did some shows last year, and released a new record this year. Like I said, it's been some of the best received stuff that I have done. It's great stuff.

MT: What does Richard say about Howard Stern behind his back?
TO: He says nothing but great stuff! He really respects Howard. This is a dream job for him. Here's the thing about Richard. He is just so much fun to be with, and kind of a normal guy to hang out with. But he's not a normal guy at all! I always say that Richard is going to be a writer for a TV show, or Saturday Night Live. He is a great and funny guy.

MT: You also find time to play with the cover bands, HAIL! and Dio Disciples. Do you feel pressure singing the Dio songs with his band?
TO: No, I don't. Wendy Dio is my Manager, and I was friends with Ronnie. I was friends with all of the guys in his band. We're not a tribute band, or even a cover band. We are celebrating Ronnie's music. We're not trying to imitate. I don't sound like him, or look like him. I feel pressure to sing well, but not to sound like Ronnie. That's a show where a lot of people show up not knowing what to expect. People are crying every night, and a lot of them leave thinking, "Wow, this was something else."

MT: Who do you burden with your scheduling?
TO: I handle a lot of it. Wendy is my Manager and she does a lot as well, but there is stuff that I like to handle myself. This year solo, I start in Mexico, then I do all of May in Australia, all of September and part of October in Europe, all of November in South America. The funny thing is that I actually go into each year hoping that I get shows. I've got to pay the bills!

MT: Musically speaking, what are your top three existing music projects in order of priority?
TO: Solo/Beyond Fear would be first. They are kind of the same. You wouldn't think that I would put this next, but Dio Disciples. I just get some kind of feeling when I play with them. It has meaning. I would clear my schedule to tour all year with that band. It's not the money. Financially solo is the way to go for me. I get paid with Dio Disciples, but I get paid triple to do something solo. Next would be CWOTD with Richard.

MT: We shouldn't neglect the discussing the "Ripper Owens Tap House" you have recently opened in Akron.
TO: It a great place! It's a sports bar/rock bar, it's called, "Ripper Owens Tap House, A Rockin' Sports Eatery." We have a bunch of music memorabilia. Guitars from KK, Glenn, Dimebag, Chris Caffery and more. Tons of drum stuff. All of it is associated with me. Photos of me from around the world with my friends in the bands I was touring with. One of the things on the menu is, "The World Tour of Wings," that is a neat concept. It consists of my travels around the world, and each wing flavor tells a story. It's a great restaurant with great entertainment. It's a small place, which will seat about 160, but I have a lot of my friends come in and play. Sebastian Bach came in to watch the Super Bowl this year. Faster Pussycat, Geoff Tate, L.A. Guns, have all played there. Eddie Trunk did a book signing there. It's just a great place. Our motto is, "We Treat Everybody Like a Rock Star."

MT: Jumping in to some personal questions, do you have a financial advisor?
TO: No.

MT: Are you registered to vote? Will you be voting in November (2012)? Who for?
TO: Yes. Yes. I am undecided.

MT: You have played with some amazing guitar players. Who is the best?
TO: Glenn Tipton and Yngwie.

MT: Do you smoke cigarettes?
TO: No.

MT: If you wake up the morning of a gig with a terrible sore throat, what is your quick fix?
TO: A lot of water, and try to get more sleep.

MT: What was your drug of choice back in the day?
TO: I really never had a drug of choice.

MT: If you took a drug test today, what would it tell us?
TO: That I am totally clean.

MT: Craziest Groupie story?
TO: There really isn't any. I hear these other bands tell crazy groupie stories, but I don't have any. I was always a pretty shy guy, and I didn't go out after the show.

MT: What is your opinion of "Meet 'n Greets"?
TO: Listen, I don't end the show and say, "All right! Let's go do the Meet 'n Greet!" But, you do them. It's part of the deal. Yngwie doesn't do any. He doesn't sign stuff. I'm from the school of Ronnie James Dio and Judas Priest where if you have to sign out in the rain, that's what you do.

MT: When you're on tour, how much do you get for your food per diem each day?
TO: That depends on the tour - $30-$40 a day, usually. Back in the Priest days, I would get $50. With Yngwie I get zero.

MT: Is there a band that you have toured with who you did not get along with?
TO: No. I have gotten along with everybody. If you can't get along with me, there is something wrong with you.

MT: Who are you listening to these days, or who are you listening to in your car?

TO: I listen to a lot of Black Sabbath with Dio. I listen to a lot of Rainbow, and Dio in general. But in the car, it's my kids' music, like Pink or Katy Perry.

MT: Who is the most over-rated musician in rock'n'roll today?
TO: Lou Reed.

MT: What is the most eccentric thing on your rider?
TO: I really don't have anything crazy. Probably sugarless gum.

MT: Have you ever been afraid for your safety while on stage performing?
TO: Yes. I used to have nightmares with Judas Priest, that if someone wanted Rob back that they would just kill me.

MT: What was the first expensive item you bought from your first big pay day?
TO: A used Jaguar.

MT: Who is the one person that you run into knowing you're going to have a long night of partying ahead of you?
TO: Phil Campbell from Motorhead.

MT: Should marijuana be legalized?
TO: I don't know. I'll say, no.

MT: Should Judas Priest be in The Rock and Roll Hall of Fame?
TO: Yes!

MT: While on tour, have you ever called a city by the wrong name? Who told you that you messed up?
TO: Yes. I had played Toledo the night before, and called Toronto, Toledo. I just kind of mumbled and acted like I didn't say it, but everyone told me they heard it after the show.

MT: When you sing in the car or shower, is it typically your songs that you sing?
TO: Yes, because I am usually learning songs for an upcoming tour.

MT: If it were a simple process, would you remove any of your tattoos?
TO: No.

MT: The best rock album ever produced?
TO: I like *Screaming for Vengeance.*

MT: What advice would you provide to a player who wants to play rock music for a living?
TO: Go to college. Take the music serious. Your goal should be to blow people away every night.

MT: What are you working on now?
TO: Check out my Facebook and my website www.tipripperowens.com to see what I am doing. You can also follow me on twitter @timripperowens

Ripper performing with Hail! in 2011

Eddie on the set of That Metal Show, New York City,
September, 2009. Photo by Ron Akiyama.

Eddie Trunk

Hard Rock/Heavy Metal Media Personality

Host/Co-Producer, That Metal Show

Eddie Trunk Rocks Q104 NYC/syndicated

Eddie Trunk Live Sirius XM Channel 39

MT: When was your birthdate?
ET: August 8, 1964.

MT: The city you were raised in?
ET: Madison, New Jersey.

MT: Do you still live in New Jersey?
ET: Yes. I have been a lifelong New Jersey resident.

MT: Did you graduate high school?
ET: Yes, in 1982.

MT: Marital status?
ET: Married.

MT: Any kids?
ET: Two children.

MT: When did you first realize that you had a love for hard rock music?
ET: The first time I heard the Raspberries, "Go All the Way" on the radio. The sound of distorted guitars coming through an AM radio in the back seat of my parent's car, it made my hair stand up. I thought that was pretty cool. That was the first time my ears had heard real crunchy rock music.

MT: Did you learn a musical instrument growing up?
ET: I played drums very early on in my school band. I took drum lessons, but I never stayed committed to it. I didn't have the patience

and the discipline, I guess, to really commit to it. So, I never really learned how to play. But, I did take lessons.

MT: Who was your first concert?
ET: Kiss and special guest, Piper – which was Billy Squier's first band at Madison Square Garden, December 16, 1977.

MT: In 1981 in Madison, New Jersey, you penned a music column in your high school paper, Sharps & Flats. What did the column consists of?
ET: For the most part, it was reviews of albums. It really wasn't anything beyond that. There were probably about six or eight that I did total. A lot of what I was writing about was new rock that I was into at the time, which would have been around 1980, or 1981. A few I remember were *Mechanix* by UFO, *Standing Hampton* by Sammy Hagar, and *Rock in a Hard Place* by Aerosmith.

MT: Your first job was at a record store. What impact did that experience have at diversifying your music knowledge?
ET: A tremendous amount. At the time, it was a dream job for me. Just being around music for a living was something that I had strived to do. So, being around it, selling it, recommending it to people, playing it in the store - it was really what I wanted to do at the time. As a kid coming out of high school, getting that job was like the ultimate gig! (laughs) It was a lot of fun, and it taught me a lot. Some music I wasn't necessarily a fan of, but working there gave me some appreciation for it, and educated me on it. To this day, people are sometimes surprised when I know about some Pop stuff, and other genres of music. Even though it is not what I personally love, working in the record store really helped shape that.

MT: Your boss at the record store broadcasted an illegal radio station from his basement, and allowed you to make a demo tape that ended up landing you your first radio gig at WDHA in Dover, New Jersey. What did the tape consists of, and do you still possess a copy of the demo tape?
ET: I still have the tape somewhere…it's on open reel. (laughs) So, I don't know if the tape is even still physically playable. I really should do something with it, and see if it's even salvageable. It was mostly me talking up records. The guy who I did this with, his interest in radio was completely different than mine. My interest was fully about playing and sharing these bands that I loved with other people. He was

much more into Top 40 radio - that sort of delivery. Big echoey voice effects, talking up records right to the post, all that sort of stuff. As a result, the tape I did reflected that. I also recall that I did a commercial. I think I did a live spot for the *New York Times*. I think the reason I got the opportunity at WDHA was for two reasons: the idea to do a metal show, which was something no one else was doing. And, they noticed that I really put forth the effort in trying to land the job. I think the tape showed how committed I was.

MT: You started the Metal Mania radio show in 1983 on WDHA. Who were some of the bands you were playing at the time? Were there any perks to that job?
ET: 1983 was a pretty big year. You had the first Metallica record come out. You had Quiet Riot, *Metal Health*, Def Leppard, *Pyromania*. I was on those records from day one. I was still working at the record store at the time, and the owners from the radio station would come in. I would push them, and say, "Look at these records." It's hard to believe now that Metallica, Quiet Riot, and Def Leppard were such heavy bands that stations didn't know what to do with them at the time, but in reality they were. Those three records I point to all the time as being very pivotal in him saying, "All right. Why don't you play some of this stuff and see what kind of reaction we get." As for perks, I was getting nothing more than I was already getting from working at the record store. Back then, if you worked in a record store, you were really being taken care of by the labels. If you wanted to go to a concert, the tickets were there the next day. If you needed a copy of an album, they would send a promo over. So, adding radio to the mix really didn't change the level of perks.

MT: You worked at the record store during the week, and WDHA on the weekends for nine years. During this time, you also served a brief stint as Vice President of Megaforce Records. Did you sign anyone big to Megaforce?
ET: The first act that I had a hand in bringing in was Ace Frehley. I was always a Kiss fan growing up, and the owner of the company, Jonny Z, was not a Kiss fan. Although I loved the metal that they were putting out - Anthrax and Metallica and all that - I thought it would be cool to have the company lean a little bit towards more air playable music as well. I mentioned to Jonny that Ace was out there, and that it could be a big coup for the company if we could land him. We went on a search to find him, and ended up signing him. So, that was the first act that I was directly involved with from an A&R capacity. I had a

small hand in bringing in King's X at the time, but outside of that, the other acts that I worked with really didn't have all that much success. I signed a band called Icon, and another named Prophet, neither of which did the business that we all hoped they would.

MT: Struggling to make ends meet, you pursued your dream of breaking into the New York City market. In 1992, you sent an air check to the newly formatted, Q104.3. Were you surprised when you received a phone call from them?
ET: Shocked, really, because I didn't put all that much into submitting that tape. New York was only 35 miles from where I lived and where WDHA was, but it was another world away to me due to the market size alone. We were broadcasting to a couple of counties in New Jersey vs. a New York station that covers three states. It was something that was just really a long shot, and I didn't put much into it making the tape. So I was completely and utterly shocked when I got a call from submitting it.

MT: You went from a 3,000 watt station at WDHA, to a 50,000 watt station at Q104 in the biggest market in the country as a classic rock DJ. You stayed at Q104 until 1998 when you were hired by WNEW. Why did you make the jump to WNEW?
ET: Well, the format wasn't classic rock at WDHA or Q104. It was just album rock. It was a mix of new and classic rock. But, I got the job at Q104 because at the time, they were going through a tremendous amount of upheaval, including ownership changes. It was a station that could not get a foothold in the market. I survived a bunch of changes, then around 1998, a new program director wanted to bring in one of his own guys, and let me go. At that point, I briefly went back to DHA for a few months, and that's when WNEW called. WNEW was a legendary rock station in New York for decades. They were going through a lot of changes as well, and were trying to become a little more contemporary. I did a little bit of everything at WNEW, as I have at most stations that I've worked at. Although being on-air has always been my favorite thing, I was always willing to chip in wherever I needed to. It was important for me just to stay on the air in New York. Once I got a taste of the New York market, it was important to do whatever I had to stay on. That was the idea behind it.

MT: In 2002, you were also hired by XM satellite radio. Did you appreciate that you could use profanity on air if you wanted?

ET: That was not really such a big deal for me. Even to this day, if I get worked up I may curse, but I never do it for effect, or just because I can do it. Whenever possible, I always try to do live radio. In this day and age, that is actually very rare, believe it or not. One of the downsides to doing live radio on terrestrial broadcasts is that you do have that issue with the FCC. So the biggest relief was that if I had a guest on the air with me, I didn't have to worry about jumping on the delete button if they said something out of line.

MT: You stayed at WNEW doing your specialty metal show till they folded in 2003. How did you end up back at Q104?
ET: Well, something really important happened during my time at WNEW. I was able to talk them into letting me do the show that I had done for nine years in New Jersey, the Metal Mania show. That is a huge, huge, huge part of my story. It might not sound big, but it allowed me to do something different. Carve out my own niche - my own voice. I gained my own following, said what I wanted, I played what I wanted. It was extremely rare in radio, especially New York radio. So that gave me a following. It gave me an audience. That led to the show being picked up for syndication as it still is today. When WNEW basically imploded due to a stunt by Opie and Anthony, I was given a call by my old station Q104. They had really solidified in the market during the past four years, and they were aware of the audience I had built doing my hard rock/metal show. With the outcry that the show would be gone due to the demise of WNEW, they asked me to come back and do the show for them. That's the way it has been ever since.

MT: Also around this time, you got a job with VH1 Classic being one of the first hosts of "Hangin' With". Is it true that there is one show that never aired?
ET: There was one show that never aired. It was with Zakk Wylde. It was back in Zakk's drinking days. He had come in off his rocker. He started to rearrange the set, and he got crazy and belligerent with a lot of people on the set. I knew Zakk well, even at this point, so I knew how to roll with Zakk and knew what he was about. It didn't faze me at all. I kind of laughed at it, but some of the people there had no idea of the Zakk Wylde Experience! (laughs) They were kind of blown away by it. They got really upset by it, and some of the things he said, and how he handled himself. It just was a train wreck. It could have, and still could be edited to be some pretty crazy TV, but I don't own it and I

don't have it to do that with. But, that was the only one that I ever did that never made it on air.

MT: You had pitched your own heavy metal television show numerous times, and in 2008, "That Metal Show" was born. How satisfying was that?
ET: It was huge. I had always asked VH1 Classic to let me have my own voice. To not be controlled, not be told what to say, not be told who to interview, and not be told what to play. To me, that is what it's all about. That's not from an ego standpoint…it's just from a creative standpoint. But at the time, the people at VH1 Classic had very rigid rules. It was literally very scripted. Around 2006, VH1 Classic was imploded. A lot of people don't know that. They cut everybody. The studio was closed, and everybody was let go. So, it was during the next couple years that I worked on the network when they started to re-launch, to some degree. I asked them to let me do the TV show and let me bring in my friends. Let me talk how we want, say what we want and let me do my show. Those conversations turned into the birth of "That Metal Show". By far, it was one of the biggest moments of my career. Not just because I was going to have my own show and do things the way I wanted to, but because I had bounced back from having been let go. To get back on the channel after everything that had went down, and reestablish myself on television again, I was ecstatic.

Q104 studio, New York City, September 2010.
Photo by Ron Akiyama.

MT: Did VH1 have any opposition to hiring your co-hosts, and friends, Jim Florentine and Don Jamieson?

ET: Well, they didn't know who they were at first. The one thing I was told throughout the evolution of the show was that they didn't want just me as the host. What was funny, in retrospect, was that the new regime at VH1 had seen the stuff I had done with the old VH1 Classic. They took that as me. They didn't realize that I was being told what to say, what to play, how to act. They assumed I was a very serious guy that couldn't take a joke. Based on that, they wanted to bring in some other elements to mix it up a bit so that it wouldn't be so serious. I told them, "Guys, I'm not serious. That's just how I was being directed." Needless to say, I had to make it work. Don and Jim had done a series of hidden camera videos called, "Meet the Creeps". They would mess with people behind the scenes in these videos, and some of the people they messed with were rock bands. At that point they were hanging out a lot with me on the radio show anyway. I asked them for a copy of their DVDs in hopes of getting them a meeting, and to get them in the door. VH1 didn't know either of them as stand up comics, but they looked at the material, they met with us, they liked them, and realized the chemistry was there. We shot a pilot, and here we still are.

MT: You have been critical on the show of VH1's lack of financial support of "That Metal Show". Given the show's success, why do you think that is?

ET: Because it's on VH1 Classic. People have to realize that there is an enormous difference in budgets and operating funds between VH1 and VH1 Classic. The operating budgets for VH1 Classic, which is a digital cable channel vs. VH1 proper - the home of all of your reality shows - is *completely* different. Because our show is so bare bones, some people feel that it adds to the charm of it. I get that, but there is also a side of me that wishes we could clear music publishing and some of the other problems that we have. (laughs) They are good sports about it. At least they let us goof on it.

MT: Who books the guests for the show?

ET: In large part, I do. It's a huge part of what I do behind the scenes. I do it in conjunction with the network, and they also have to approve everything. But I would say a huge percentage of the guests that have appeared on the show have directly fallen on me.

MT: Do the guests on the show get paid?
ET: The musicians that play on the show do. They get paid a union fee. The guests who sit on the show and are interviewed do not get paid. That is very standard in talk television shows. In some instances, they will be put up for a night or flown in, but even that is very rare. They reason we moved the show from New York to Los Angeles was to alleviate a lot of that. 90% of our guests live in LA, so that is why even though we are east coast based, we go to LA to do the show.

MT: Tell us two guests on the show that were feeling no pain during the filming?
ET: Marilyn Manson who was drinking absinthe the entire time, and Lemmy. Lemmy is always drinking his jack and coke, but Lemmy is a guy who has been drinking his whole life, but he doesn't show it.

MT: Have you had a guest on the show that is not welcome back?
ET: No. None that I can think of.

Eddie on the set of That Metal Show, September 2009.
Photo by Ron Akiyama

MT: How are the questions developed for the "Stump the Trunk" portion of the show?

ET: It's a mix of things. It is questions that come in from the audience, and it's also questions that audience members are given. If you see audience members looking at cards that is because they have been assigned that question by the staff. The reason why that is done is that we found out very early on that if we let people just ask whatever they wanted to, they would ask things so out of left field. We had people that would come up and ask about demos, and their bands, and their friend's bands that had never even put out a record. There had to be some kind of control put into place. That's why the questions are always looked over by somebody on our staff.

MT: You have been very outspoken about The Rock and Roll Hall of Fame doing a poor job of acknowledging the hard rock/heavy metal genre. Have you received any response from them?
ET: Yes, the president of the Hall of Fame was on my radio show a few months ago. He reached out to me. He was aware of how vocal I've been about it, and wanted to give his side of things. He stepped up enough to come on the air and debate and discuss it with me. So, we had that conversation but, it really didn't lead to all that much because at the end of the day, his point was that he doesn't have a vote. He is not involved in the voting end. He did shine some light on the process and how they work there, but they are fully aware of how I feel and have made some overtures to me over the years.

MT: Has VH1 ever asked you to "tone it down" regarding your opinion of the HOF?
ET: No! To their credit they have not. That kind of goes back to what I said about having a show that is really your show, and being able to say what you want. The old VH1 certainly would have, but now they are fine with it. They understand that it is an important issue to me, and that it means a lot to me to expose it. No, they have never tried to reel me in from it.

MT: You have mentioned that Gene and Paul from Kiss, and Ozzy Osbourne have never done the show, but you would love to have them on. Why do you think Gene and Paul are hesitant?
ET: For a couple reasons. They know that I am an extremely educated fan. Most artists are much happier doing interviews with people who read their bio five minutes before they walked up, and will accept - and not challenge - anything they say. Also, I think, unfortunately, they are probably not happy with what I have said about Kiss in terms of what they do these days. I have been a Kiss fan my whole life, and I think

that anyone who has been a fan of any band realizes there is usually something in a band's history that you didn't like. I don't have a problem saying that I don't like what they are doing now. I think that is a large part of it. I hope that someday they will come on and debate, and discuss how I feel. That's what it's about, having the dialogue. But at this point I think they know that I have my position, and they don't want to come in and challenge it.

MT: And Ozzy?
ET: That would be a question for Sharon Osbourne. In the case of Gene and Paul, I think that it's mostly Paul. I have an idea what he probably thinks, because I know what I have said. In the Ozzy situation, I don't think that Ozzy has a clue about me, to be honest with you. It's clearly Sharon Osbourne and we honestly don't know. Again, I have been outspoken on a few things that have happened with Ozzy over the years that she has been behind, but they were all things that he himself had issues with. It has to be something in her head, and I don't know what it is because I don't know the woman. I think it's unfortunate though, because people want to see these artists on a show where the hosts really are fans and know the music. Instead they go on shows that don't even play their music, make fun of them after they leave, or go on shows that their audience doesn't ever watch. It's unfortunate, but I see it happen all the time.

MT: In 2010, you released the book, *Eddie Trunk's Essential Hard Rock and Heavy Metal*. Did you enjoy the book writing process?
ET: I did! It was much more work than I ever thought it was going to be. I am going to do a second book. I just need to get my head in a place where I am ready to tackle it. It was a lot of work, I learned a lot about the process, but the most rewarding thing about having done it is that it sold extremely well. People genuinely really, really liked it. I hear from my audience all the time if there is something I do that they don't like, and I welcome all opinions. The book is one of the things that I don't think I heard a negative. Everything was completely positive. People truly loved it.

MT: At this point in your career, is there an artist that intimidates you to interview?
ET: I don't know about being intimidated. But, I have interviewed Axl Rose twice. It's not necessarily intimidation, well, it is I guess if you look at it from the standpoint of being worried that if you say something, and he's going to walk out. Just because he's volatile. It's

not intimidation in the sense that, "Oh my god, this guy is going to get up and punch me in the face." It's just that you have to be careful of how you say things, and what you say.

MT: Has an artist that you are friends with ever called and asked your opinion or advice before they made a big career decision?
ET: Sure, absolutely. The one that comes to mind most immediately is Ace Frehley. Ace and I have a long, long history together. We still talk and we are still friends. He will call me and ask, "What do you think of this?" Even in his own book, he makes a comment saying something like, "As usual, Ed Trunk gave me good advice." Or something to that effect. Ace is a guy that I certainly have that sort of relationship with.

MT: When was the last time that you wanted a back stage pass to a show and were unsuccessful in obtaining one?
ET: It's very rare that that happens, but it actually just happened recently with Van Halen for their current tour (2012). I'm not one of these groupie-type guys that needs to be back there to eat and drink for free. I am always looking for ways to make contact to grow my shows, and by that I mean that Eddie Van Halen and the Van Halen camp is without question one of the most heavily requested artists for That Metal Show. So, I was trying to make some inroads, not necessarily with the band, but people that I knew in their camp to try to facilitate getting them on the show. It wasn't anything personal that I couldn't get back there. It was just that they have a very tight ship. Unless you are in the inner circle, and you are personal friends, you're not going back. There is no hanging out back there, and I completely respect that.

MT: At the 2012 Rock and Roll Hall of Fame induction ceremony, Steven Adler wore a very visible "That Metal Show" t-shirt. How proud did you feel when you saw that?
ET: It was awesome! I just spoke to him about that on my radio show. It really surprised me. Steven is such a rock 'n' roll fan. Such a fan of, as crazy as it sounds, mine and what I do. He really, really blew us all away by doing that. I have been so vocal against the Hall of Fame, and for him to be on stage on one of the biggest nights of his life representing my show was pretty amazing. He said to me on my radio show, that he considers me the modern day Don Kirshner. (laughs) He said that he wanted to represent, and do that for my support. It meant a lot to me, and all the folks who work on That Metal Show. I was really happy to see him do that, and thankful.

MT: Let's jump to some personal questions. Are you registered to vote? Who will you be voting for in the 2012 Presidential election?
ET: I am registered as an independent. I haven't made my decision who for, but I lean conservative in my views.

MT: Do you smoke cigarettes?
ET: No, never.

MT: How often are you recognized in public?
ET: In a rock concert environment it's pretty intense, in a good way. I am thankful for that. Walking through the aisles of a supermarket or down the street? A few times. Every once in a while someone will yell out, "That Metal Show!" or "Stump the Trunk!" (laughs). It's nice, but it's nothing to the degree if I'm at a place where there is a common audience for what I do.

MT: What is the best perk you receive with your job?
ET: Probably the access to the shows. I can't remember the last time I paid for a concert ticket. Most of the time I drive right back, circumvent parking, go see the guys, and sit in a great spot. I really appreciate that, and I try to keep that in perspective. I never overdo it. I never ask for other people, besides a guest and me. I'm very respectful of it, and I understand it's how these guys make their living now, more than ever. For me, the biggest perk overall is still making a living doing what I love.

MT: If you took a drug test today, what would it tell us?
ET: Nothing. I have never done a drug in my life. It's something that a lot of people are pretty amazed at when I tell them that. I have an occasional drink, a couple a month would be a lot for me. It's just something that I never got caught up in. My parents raised me well. If you really think about it, it's pretty remarkable because I spent my whole life in the music industry and never did drugs.

MT: Do you follow sports?
ET: The Giants in the NFL are by far my favorite sport and team. I am a Mets fan in baseball, a Rangers fan in hockey, and a Nets fan in basketball.

MT: Do you have any tattoos?
ET: No, not one.

MT: Do you realize that many people consider you the "ambassador" for hard rock/heavy metal? How does that make you feel?

ET: People say that sort of stuff to me a lot, and it means a lot to me and I am really grateful that people feel that strongly about what I have done. I have certainly put the work in to get to that point, and I have stayed consistent with what I do, and what I feel regarding the things that I have fought 30 years for now. So, it means a lot to me to hear that sort of reverence from my audience, and I am grateful for it. But when I hear people talk like that, or even read the quotes on the back of my book, it almost feels like at times that they are talking about someone else. One of the things I don't do is sit there and smell the roses, if you will. I always have tunnel vision moving forward, and am thinking about what I can do to make this bigger or better. That's not for selfish or financial purposes, it's for the reason that I wrote the school newspaper column when I was a kid - what can I do to continue to grow and share this music with other people? That is really what it comes down to. At the end of the day, I still just consider myself a fan.

MT: What advice would you provide to someone interested in pursuing a career as a rock 'n' roll talk show host?

ET: Experience. First and foremost, experience. Just being around it. Getting that first job in a record store was a big, big thing for me. It gave me so much experience. From that it gave me contacts to get into radio. From that it gave me contacts to record companies. I was a sponge. I was learning and I was networking, and off of that little record store job, a lot of this spun off and happened. So it's just being around the business you love, being persistent without being annoying which is a very fine line and being good at what you do. Always self evaluate what you do, take criticism and have a thick skin. I was told as a little kid by a DJ at DHA, "You'll never be on the radio. You don't have the chops, or the voice." That just made me stronger. Instead of just packing my tent, it made me rally harder. When I'm told about things that I can't do, that just makes me want to prove people wrong. And that still happens to this day. You just need to learn how to manage that stuff and roll it off your back.

MT: What are you working on now?

ET: I have two radio shows, one on FM radio that is syndicated. I am constantly working to get that on more stations. It's extremely frustrating that more stations don't air it just because the TV show is so popular, but they are afraid to run the radio show which is where a lot of the TV show comes from. I also do a live show on Mondays, 3-7 pm Pacific Time on channel 39, which is called, Hair Nation on Sirius/XM radio. I don't like that branding, so it is called Trunk Nation when I am on. I do all sorts of music and talk on that. Of course, That Metal Show. And I will start working on a sequel to my book soon. And all of these things that I mentioned, I am always trying to grow them and look for new opportunities whether they be in TV or radio. I have even recently done some writing for *Classic Rock Magazine*, so I kind of went back to square one a little bit. But, so far it's been great! I wouldn't trade anything in the world for it.

Jeff Duncan, July 2010. Photo by Gregory I. Allen/GiaPhoto.us

Jeff Duncan

Lead Guitar/Vocals

Past-Odin

Present-Armored Saint, DC4

MT: When is your birthday?
JD: January 28, 1966.

MT: The city you were raised in?
JD: Los Angeles, California.

MT: The city you currently reside?
JD: Los Angeles, California.

MT: Did you graduate high school?
JD: No.

MT: Do you rent or own the place you call home?
JD: Rent.

MT: How big is it, and how much is your rent?
JD: It's a two-bedroom, two-story apartment. I pay $800 a month.

MT: Is your current home the biggest that you lived in?
JD: They all have been pretty much the same size.

MT: Do you have any roommates?
JD: Yes, one.

MT: Relationship status?
JD: Single.

MT: Any kids?
JD: No.

MT: When did you pick up your first guitar?

JD: I was six. My dad was a guitar player and songwriter. He actually had a hit in the early 60s, but he would write songs and play guitar at home. I would just go in there and watch him. I was fascinated. He would be singing but I would be watching his fingers on the guitar. He said to me, "You really like the guitar, don't you?" So he put me up on the bed and put this big giant guitar in my lap. He showed me an E chord and I took it from there.

MT: Do you remember the first time you thought you were good enough to make a living playing guitar?

JD: No, I really never looked at it like that. I always looked at a guitar as a way of creating songs. I guess I got that from my dad. Early on when I put a band together, it was never about the money. I had heroes like Zeppelin and Van Halen, but I never wanted to be them. Even in the very early stages of Odin, we had a guitar player named Brad Parker. He was older than me, and was saying that we had to do this and we had to do that and all this promoting stuff, and he was good at it. I asked him," Why?" And he said, "So we can make it." I seriously didn't know what he meant. Not to be falsely humble, but I was always into excelling and improving. I still don't think that I consider myself a 'good enough' guitar player. So, I don't know if that ever even happened.

MT: You were a founding member of Odin which had a huge presence on the Sunset Strip in the 80s. How old were you when the band formed, and how did it happen?

JD: I actually joined a band in seventh grade called The Termites. We weren't very good. Early on, the drummer ended up getting grounded for two weeks and couldn't rehearse, so we kicked him out of the band and my brother, Shaun, became our drummer. Our childhood friend, Art Garza, was singing for us at the time, and we decided to change the band's name to Tempest. We started playing a lot of backyard parties, but then we learned there was another band called, Tempest. Our bass player at the time found the name Odin in a book of baby names. We liked how it sounded and changed the band's name to Odin. We became a popular keg party band and gigged a good amount. Then in eighth grade, I met Aaron Samson. He was such a better bass player and we hit it off, so we booted the other guy out. Fast forward to high school, Art moves to San Jose with his girlfriend, gets married, and quits the band. That's when I met Brad Parker (guitar). We used to rehearse at Art's house and since he had moved to San Jose, we had no place to practice. Brad had a nice studio in his garage, and I told the other guys that we should have Brad join the band because he had a place to rehearse. Brad joined the band, but we needed a singer. So, we put an ad in The Recycler, and Randy 'O' was one of the guys who auditioned. Oddly enough, our first legitimate club gig on the Strip was opening for Armored Saint. Randy 'O' decided that he didn't like Brad, so we kicked him (Brad) out and it became us four. That was the Odin that became known.

MT: How old were you when you had that first legit gig opening for Armored Saint?
JD: 17.

MT: How did you skirt the fact that you were under 21?
JD: Back then, especially the Troubadour, it was kind of like the Wild West. Nobody asked. We just showed up looking like rockers, and nobody asked questions.

MT: Was your family supportive? Would they come to your gigs?
JD: Yes, very supportive. In fact, in the early days of Odin, my dad managed us.

MT: So you are a teenager, playing the Sunset Strip during the peak of the metal movement, and Penelope Spheeris approached Odin about being in her documentary, "Decline of Western Civilization, The Metal Years." How did that happen?
JD: There was a guy who worked with the band very closely, Doug Campbell. He got the call, and I'm not sure how she even knew who we were. That was a weird period for the band as we were on our last leg. The band wasn't really happy. As a matter of fact, I went to the premier of that movie as a member of Armored Saint.

MT: What was your payday to participate?
JD: I honestly don't remember. I remember having a nice wad of cash in my pocket from it, but I don't remember how much it was.

MT: Do you remember the filming, or were you in an altered state?
JD: Probably a little of both. I remember doing it, but we were all a little crazy and out of control at the time.

MT: How did you feel when the documentary came out?

JD: I used to not like talking about it. It was a painful subject for me and for a lot of people. I didn't like how we were portrayed. In the end though, it was a very positive experience. Over the years I have been approached by many people saying, 'I know you from the movie, and that band was great, and what happened to the band?' It's just too bad Odin was on their last leg at the time, and even though it gave us a lot of exposure, we were done trying with that band. Remember, we were a very popular LA band consistently the whole time we were together. We saw so many bands pass us up. We saw Guns N' Roses pass us up. Warrant, Poison, and many others pass us up. We would still sell out. We were still huge, but we just couldn't get out of that Sunset Strip scene.

MT: The late Bill Gazzarri was a fan of Odin. How was your relationship with him? What was he like?

JD: He was great. He was so into the band, and very fair. In Odin's later years, we did a lot of shows at Gazzarri's. The main reason was that he would give us such a good deal that we would make money, he would make money. He was very fair. He was just an old school lover of rock & rollers. He was a unique individual. I was very sad when he died.

MT: After Odin disbanded, you joined Armored Saint and went on tour playing alongside your friend, David Prichard. What was that like?

JD: It was great. I had never really done any extensive touring, so I was pretty green. I was 22 years old and was it great to be with all of them. Odin and Armored Saint had played a lot together on Sunset, so it wasn't very difficult as these guys were already my friends.

MT: How close were you and David?

JD: Dave and I got along very well. He was the instigator for bringing me into the band. He liked the way I played, and felt that I was the right guy to be in that band.

MT: Where were you when you found out that he was sick?

JD: He had a party at his house. His parents would go on vacation and he would throw these huge parties. I was talking to him at the party, and he let me know that he wanted to talk with me privately. We went to different room, and he told me he had leukemia. I freaked out, and asked him if he was going to be ok. He told me, "Calm down, I'm not dead." He had a really good spirit about it the entire time. He just really fought hard. That was Dave. He was a very resilient person. And was a very headstrong kind of guy.

David Prichard and Jeff in December 1985. Recita, California

MT: Did you realize how serious it was? Was everyone close to him under the mindset that he could beat the leukemia?
JD: I didn't realize how serious it was, but it wasn't something that we thought he wouldn't get through. It didn't make sense with Dave. It was weird when he passed away because it never seemed a guy like Dave would die so young. It seemed like he would outlive everybody. He had that personality.

MT: David passed away months after being diagnosed with the disease at 26 years old. How comfortable was the band moving forward without David?
JD: Before Dave passed, I had left the band. I had some issues with drinking and drugging, and I needed to focus on cleaning myself up. So, I wasn't technically in the band when Dave passed. At the time that Dave passed, Armored Saint had no guitar players. That was the state the band was in. You have to understand that those guys in Armored Saint went to grade school together. They were childhood friends, so it was very devastating what happened to David. So, some time had passed and I got a call from John Bush. He told me that Phil (Sandoval, guitar) was going to come back to the band, and asked me to

rejoin them as well, being the band's two guitar players. I was ready to do that. At that time, I was in "Lost Boys" with Randy 'O'. It was more of his thing, and I wasn't totally satisfied, so I jumped at the chance to rejoin Armored Saint.

MT: The first Armored Saint album you were part of was *Symbol of Salvation*. Was any of David's playing on that album?
JD: The only thing on there is the guitar solo on "Tainted Past." It was actually flown in from the demo for that song. So they lifted that solo from the demo, and put his solo on that song.

MT: When you toured with Armored Saint in support of the album you opened for Dokken and others, how was the pay for those types of gigs?
JD: I don't know (laughs). I honestly don't. I was paid a salary of about $300 a week, but as far as breaking it down by gig, I don't know that. I never asked. It's just how I was at the time. I was happy to be touring and rock & rolling.

MT: In 1992, Armored Saint learned that their vocalist, John Bush, was recruited by the band, Anthrax. Did you know this was happening or were you shocked by the news?
JD: That was a tough thing. John had turned down their initial offer, but they were relentless. Eventually the offer they put on the table for him was too good to turn down. Armored Saint was having a rough time. It was the 90s. Grunge had really taken over, and we had a tough time touring. I remember the last gig we played was in Hawaii. Before we left for the trip, John told Joey (Vera, bass) and I that he was joining Anthrax. So we played this gig in Hawaii with Overkill. It was an off-the-hook show, and I remember walking off stage, looking at the crowd saying,"Wow, this is over." John and I were roommates for about a year after he joined Anthrax, so there were no hard feelings.

MT: Do you have a favorite song to play live with Armored Saint?
JD: Oh, yeah. There are a lot of them. "Pay Dirt," "Book of Blood" and "Stricken by Fate" are my favorites.

MT: Your friend, Randy 'O', from Odin told me that he thinks you are one of the 10 best guitar players in the world. How does that feel when you hear such a compliment?

JD: That is a really sweet thing to say. I don't necessarily claim that, but that is very nice to hear. Randy 'O' and I have been through a lot together, and I'm glad that we are now closer than we have ever been.

MT: In your opinion, who are the top three guitar players living today?
JD: Eddie Van Halen, Tony Iommi, and Michael Schenker.

MT: Jumping back into your timeline, in the late 90s, you started DC4. Is DC4 your priority now?
JD: It's definitely the one that I am most active with.

MT: The other guitar player in DC4 is a talented guy who was picked up by Dio at the age of 17, Rowan Robertson. Who is a better guitar player? You or Rowan?
JD: That's a funny question. I would probably say he is, and he would probably say that I am. People ask me all the time if we fight over who is going to do the guitar solos, and I say, "Yeah! I want him to do them, and he wants me to do them!" (laughs).

MT: Have you ever auditioned for a band and not got the gig?
JD: I have never auditioned for anybody. Wait, that's not true. I auditioned in a studio with Dave and Joey for Armored Saint. They put on a drum machine and we jammed "Can U Deliver" for about a minute. Then we went and got a beer.

MT: Do you have a favorite hangout on Sunset?
JD: I don't go down there that much, but for a long time I used to hang out at the Cat Club which was the tiny club next to The Whisky. It's not there anymore, but I really liked that place.

Jeff Duncan promo photo, April 2011.
Photo by Gregory I. Allen/GiaPhoto.US

MT: The Sunset Strip has changed a lot since the 80s. How does Pay to Play work?
JD: Some of the clubs now hand the bands 50 tickets when they book them. The tickets have to be sold by the night they perform. Basically, they have to show up to sound check with $500 or they don't play.

MT: How much of your current income is music related?
JD: About 75%.

MT: How often do you gig presently with Armored Saint and/or DC4?
JD: DC4 gigs, about every six weeks. Armored Saint doesn't gig that often. We only go out on short tours.

MT: Armored Saint played the Key Club over the summer (2011) in July. Does a gig like that pay well?
JD: Probably about $6,000.

MT: Do you receive publishing monies from Odin, Armored Saint or DC4?
JD: Yes, all three.

MT: Are the bands publishing rights split evenly in Armored Saint and DC4?
JD: They're split evenly in DC4. In Armored Saint, they're not even. I don't remember what my exact cut is, but I do get a percentage of everything.

MT: To date, what band have you earned the most income from?
JD: Armored Saint.

MT: What is a typical annual earning amount for you?
JD: It's tough to say because it changes every year. It's probably $25,000.

MT: What do you do outside of gigging to make ends meet?
JD: Teach guitar.

MT: Do you have endorsement deals? How do they work?
JD: Yes, I have deals now with Krank Amps, ESP Guitars, D'Addario strings, Seymour Duncan pickups, Mystarsound Cables, Stage Ninja,

and TonePros. I use their products and try to mention them during interviews.

MT: When was the last time you set an alarm to wake up to, and why?
JD: Six months ago for an interview.

MT: What kind of car do you drive?
JD: I drive a 1995 Chevy Astro Van.

MT: Do you have a favorite car that you have owned?
JD: I had a 1966 Dodge Dart that I really liked.

MT: Are you registered to vote? If so, who will you vote President in 2012?
JD: I am registered to vote. Obama.

MT: If it were a simple process, would you have any of your tattoos removed?
JD: No.

MT: What makes you laugh?
JD: Dark humor. The more unsavory and wrong a joke can be, I will laugh my ass off (laughs).

MT: Who is the best musician you have ever played with?
JD: Billy Sheehan.

MT: Who was the worst musician?
JD: I used to do these jams at the Cat Club all of the time. I remember one night we were jamming, and a guy came up who was playing drums for Yngwie at the time. I don't remember his name. So, we decide to go into "Tush," a typical bar song. When the drums came in, he played a double bass thrash pattern the whole way through. I couldn't wait for it to end.

MT: What rock/metal band is going to be the next big thing?
JD: I don't know (long pause). There is this talented kid that plays with this band called, "Age of Evil" out of Arizona. The guitar player is really young, but you're going to hear a lot about this kid. He is really good.

MT: How many cigarettes do you smoke a day?
JD: I smoke about a pack a day.

MT: How is your health?
JD: I feel great. I am not suffering from anything.

MT: Is there a person you like least in Rock & Roll?
JD: Not a person, but a type of person. Anybody that isn't willing to take time, even three seconds, for a fan. That, I just don't understand.

MT: Is there anyone who could make you star struck?
JD: Paul McCartney.

MT: If you could turn back to a particular year during your life, what year would you choose and why.
JD: 1985. It was a very good, carefree…and ignorance is bliss time. As far as state of mind and personally, I am much happier now. But, that time was a very special period.

MT: If you could write your own ticket and play lead guitar in any band, who would you want to play for?
JD: There was a time that I could have answered that question very easily. That answer would have been Dio. I would probably say the Foo Fighters now.

MT: Tell us about your worst sexual experience?
JD: Okay (laughs). This is like a David Lynch movie. It's about 1987, and I had been partying all night. A group of us go down to Venice Beach. By now it's about 11am, and I meet this blonde girl. She was drunk too. So we hit it off and she invites me to her place. When we get there she says she'll be right back, and goes into this room and closes the door. When she comes back, we start going at it. I mean I am nailing this girl. So as I'm nailing her I look to my left and see this little girl with Down syndrome watching us. It was her daughter. I just freaked out, and threw my clothes on, and got out of there. I never saw that girl again. It was really fucked up.

MT: Do you typically wear protection?
JD: Yeah. That's why I don't have any kids!

MT: What's the scariest STD you ever caught?

JD: I only caught something once. Something called, Urethritis. Just kind of a drip. I got a shot and it went away.

MT: How many times have you had sex in your backstage dressing room?
JD: I don't know. Maybe three times.

MT: How many women have you been with?
JD: Oh, I don't know. 200?

MT: What country in the world has the hottest women, best food and best geographic scenery?
JD: Hottest woman - Sweden. Best food, Greece. I think Canada has some beautiful landscape.

MT: When you're on tour, how much do you get for your food per diem each day?
JD: It depends. It's gig by gig. Sometimes you get $40, sometimes $15.

MT: When is the last time you paid for or changed your own guitar strings?
JD: The last time I paid for strings was 10 years ago. I just changed my own guitar strings last night.

MT: What band are you listening to in your car right now?
JD: Pantera.

MT: Who is the most overrated musician in rock'n'roll today?
JD: Jack White. I just don't get it.

MT: If you took a drug test today, what would it tell us?
JD: It would tell you that I have a lot of nicotine and caffeine in my system. I don't drink, I don't smoke pot. I don't do anything that is mind-altering.

MT: Turn back the clock 25 years. Who was the one person that you would run into knowing you're going to have a long night of partying ahead of you?
JD: Chris Holmes.

MT: When was the last time you were blown away by a band's live performance?
JD: At the NAMM show I saw Steve Vai play. He floored me.

MT: Who is the toughest guy in rock'n'roll?
JD: James Hetfield has a pretty intense presence, but a very cool, sweet person.

MT: What is the best rock album ever produced?
JD: It would be a toss-up between Van Halen's *Fair Warning* and Black Sabbath's *Heaven and Hell*.

MT: What advice would you provide a guitarist looking to play rock music for a living?
JD: Never put making a living at guitar playing before the love of the art. The more I put into the art and creativity, the better I get at it, the better I sound and play. I see a lot of bands perform live that are too eager to become rock stars, when they should have spent that night in the rehearsal studio. Stay on top of your business, and do whatever you can to maintain control of your career.

MT: What is next for Jeff Duncan?
JD: We just started writing for DC4, and we'll have another CD out by August 2012. Armored Saint will be heading to Europe this summer (2012). Odin still pops up now and then which is really cool. Both Odin and DC4 performed on the "Monsters of Rock Cruise" in 2012.

MT: How can people get a hold of you?
JD: You can reach out to me on the DC4 or Odin Facebook Page. I'm not hard to find.

Tracii in West Springfield, Virginia. July 2009.
Photo by Robin Watts Photography.

Tracii Guns

Lead Guitar

Past-Pyhrrus, Guns N' Roses, Contraband, Killing Machine, Brides of
Destruction, Tracii Guns Bastard Blues Band, Starfuckers

Present-L.A. Guns, League of Gentlemen

MT: When was your birthdate?
TG: January 20, 1966.

MT: The city you were raised in?
TG: Hollywood, California.

MT: The city you currently reside?
TG: Hollywood, California.

MT: Did you graduate high school?
TG: I took what is called a Proficiency Test, and received a diploma.

MT: Marital status?
TG: I am single, but have had the same girlfriend for 21 years.

MT: Any kids?
TG: One boy. Jagger James Guns.

MT: When was the first time you picked up a guitar?
TG: I was five or six years old. I heard "Whole Lotta Love" on the
radio in my mom's car, and that ruined my life! I think the first photo
of me playing guitar, I'm six years old.

MT: Were you a popular kid in school?
TG: I was popular amongst my friends. I don't know how popular I
was amongst everybody. I had an outgoing personality, but I was very
shy around people that I didn't know.

MT: You participated in Guitar Ensemble class while attending Bancroft Junior High. Were there any other decent guitar players in your class?

TG: Slash was in my class. He was pretty decent! Slash and I became friends when I was around 11 years old.

MT: In the early 80s, Izzy Stradlin moved from Indiana to LA, as did Axl Rose a couple years later. Is it true that you were all roommates for a while?

TG: Yes. Izzy was playing with my singer's brother's band called, Shire. He was the bass player, and I met him at a Shire show. We became best friends right away, and he moved into my mom's house, where I was living. Axl came out a few times before he actually stayed in LA. Axl lived at my mom's house on and off for a while till Izzy moved on, and in with his girlfriend, Desi. Then Axl and I were attached at the hip for a couple years. We were all very close

MT: When you first met Axl, was he going by his original name, Bill Bailey?

TG: He was still Bill! It's weird to call him Bill. Axl just suited him so well. When people would get mad at him they would call him Bill, but Bill was a very uncomfortable thing to call him once he was Axl.

MT: You started L.A. Guns in 1982, and replaced the bands original singer with Axl Rose. How did he mesh with the other band members?

TG: He was very easy to get along with. He was excited to play live music, and excited to write music. He was a good friend, and we all had each other's back. Axl at that point in time was a real gentleman. He was a very smart and funny guy. The kind of guy you would want as a best friend.

MT: During this time, Izzy had joined the LA based band, London. Reportedly, Axl had a falling out with London's singer, Nadir D'Priest, forcing Izzy to leave London. What happened between Axl and Nadir?

TG: Actually, that was Axl sticking up for me. When Izzy joined London, we started doing a lot of shows together, as we were all supposedly friends. I am still friends with Nadir, which is weird. But Axl had seen Nadir detune my guitars before we went on, or so he claimed. But, sure enough, when I went to put my guitar on that night it was out of tune. I put the next guitar on - it was out of tune as well. So when we went on stage, Axl ripped up a London poster. There is a photo of this in Marc Canter's book. That was the beginning of all hell breaking loose between those two. Axl and Izzy were kind of humble guys, but growing up they had their share of street fights. So just because they were on the quiet side, didn't mean that they wouldn't whip somebody's butt. On the flip side, Nadir was a really tough guy. He had been in and out of jail, and was a pretty tough kid. A lot of the time I would pick up Axl from work at Tower Video, and a few times Nadir was waiting for Axl outside. They would have these quick little battles, then Nadir would run off. One day, Nadir was waiting outside with a gun! Axl is a tough motherfucker, man. He picked up a broken street sign and just whacked Nadir with it! As far as I know, that was the last time they tangled. Throughout all of that, even to this day, Nadir and I have a good relationship.

MT: Later L.A Guns Manager fired Axl. What was his reasoning?
TG: I don't even remember. It was probably over something ridiculous. We were all teenagers. It was after a gig, and we were all driving home in the same car. And Raz, our manager, just turned to Axl and said, "You're fired. You're not going to be in L.A. Guns anymore." When we got home, Raz went into his room and Axl and I sat on the couch. We both looked at each other and said, "How in the hell can he fire anybody?" By the end of the conversation, we had constructed Guns N' Roses. Also, Izzy wasn't playing in London any longer, so that was kind of the catalyst to start a new band.

MT: In 1985, with Axl and Izzy band-less, the three of you decided to start your own band, Guns N' Rose, until Duff Rose showed up. Is that how it happened?
TG: Well, that is the way we put it out there. I think that we came up with Guns N' Roses first, but then it didn't make sense. There was only one Rose, but Guns N' Roses sounded better. It was just a coincidence that Duff was going by Duff Rose when he joined the band, so Guns N' Roses made more sense at that point.

MT: What was once loosely L.A. Guns was now Guns N' Roses. Slash mentions in his biography, *Slash*, that he believed, and I quote, "Tracii and Axl had a major falling out. Tracii quit pretty soon afterward." What really happened?
TG: Axl kind of disappeared for a week in between two weekends of shows. I don't know what he was doing. Maybe I thought I knew what he was doing, but I'm not going to assume what he was doing. He had

called Izzy before sound check on the first night of two shows, and he told Izzy, "Tell Tracii to make sure that Michelle Young is on the guest list." She was a friend of ours. So he showed up at sound check at 4:00 pm, and there was no guest list turned in. He went bananas on everybody. We were all like, "Jesus Christ, who is this guy?" It certainly wasn't like Axl. It was a different person. I remember that we had a really good show that night - the place was packed. I remember Izzy and I starring across the stage at each other thinking, "What the fuck?" The vibe was just all dark and weird. The next night was the first time that Axl ever showed up late! (laughs). He really didn't show up late, he just showed up at the last minute. After the show, I remember driving home with Duff. We were talking about how all of the fighting within the band wasn't fun for anybody. The next week, I just stopped going to rehearsal. Axl would call me screaming and yelling, and then Izzy would get on the phone in a more calm voice and try to reason with me. I just wanted to have a good time. I was only 18 or 19 at the time. The band had turned into the podium for Axl to speak on stage, which is a great place to speak your mind, but the other four guys on stage wanted to play our songs. We were to the point where we were playing six songs a night rather than 12. We were definitely a tight knit unit. Nobody fucked with us when we were L.A. Guns, or Guns N' Roses. It was like, "Fuck you, this is our way. This is how we do it." Eventually we had the "Fuck you, it's my way" attitude within the band. (laughs). That is when I left and Slash came in.

MT: What was your reaction when you heard Slash had taken your spot in GNR?
TG: I figured that would be the obvious choice. He had played with everybody in the band except Duff. He was one of my closest friends, and had actually come up with the original GNR logo before he was in the band. He was a real fan of Guns N' Roses. I think that having him see the band from the audience, made him appreciate it more. As soon as he was in the band, I really started enjoying the band more. I think it worked out the best for everybody. I really do.

MT: In 1987, you reformed L.A. Guns with Phil Lewis (vocals), Steve Riley (drums), Mick Cripps (rhythm guitar), and Kelly Nickels (bass). How excited was the band when you signed with Polygram?
TG: The actual band that got the record deal was Mick, Nickey Beat, Paul Black, and I. We did all of the leg work, and built a great

following. We were at our big meeting with Polygram, and Paul Black nodded off when he was asked, "What do you hope to get out of your music career?" (laughs). That wasn't good, and it was a big surprise to me because I had no idea he was doing dope. We left the meeting and Alan Jones, our manager, says, "Guys, this isn't going to work out." And I said, "What do you mean?" and Alan said, "Well, Paul fell asleep at the meeting." And I go, "Yeah, he must be really tired." (laughs). So, Alan asked me who I would like to have sing for the band. I answered, "Robert Plant!" He obviously wanted someone a little more realistic. I asked him about Phil Lewis from Girl, and Alan not only knew him, but was friends with him. We brought Phil out here and auditioned him. He walked up to the microphone, sang three words, and I said, "You got the gig." With this change, Mick who was playing bass, wanted to play rhythm guitar. We got Kelly to play bass who was formerly in Faster Pussycat. He was in a terrible motorcycle accident, and in a half-body cast at the time. We flew him out and he played his first gig with us in this enormous cast on his lower body. His first couple gigs he sat on a chair.

MT: L.A. Guns first album, *L.A. Guns* ('88), second album, *Cocked and Loaded* ('89), and third album, *Hollywood Vampires* ('91) all went platinum and featured close to the same band line-up. Was the band at that time ever inspired by trying to keep up with GNR?
TG: No, but I remember there was an ad put together by our product development manager, Steve Cline. It said something to the effect of, "Hey, Guns N' Roses. It's L.A Guns knocking, were right behind you, we're coming up quick." I remember that it made the entire band feel really weird. Besides Axl and I wanting to punch each other, it wasn't a very competitive thing.

MT: You were a member of the side project, Contraband, with Michael Schenker and Bobby Blotzer in 1991. Did you play rhythm, and Michael played lead? How was that experience?
TG: No, it was like dueling banjos. There was a guy who played rhythm on the album, but Michael and I both played the solos. I don't think I spent more than two or three days doing that record, and I am pretty sure that Michael didn't either, but it turned out nice. The album managed to do well with just one tour date. It almost went gold! It wasn't a game changer by any means, but it was certainly a solid rock 'n' roll record. And I got to play with Michael Schenker, which was huge for me.

MT: In January of '92, Phil Lewis fired Steve Riley after L.A. Guns had toured with Skid Row. What happened?

TG: Phil had disappeared for a while. He's not the kind of guy to just bow out of something because he doesn't feel like doing it, but he had some personal stuff that he needed to take care of. I was totally cool with it. Then something happened that I didn't see. During that tour, I guess Steve had hit Phil with a newspaper at breakfast. I mean, really gave him one. No one said anything to me till we got home from the tour. Eventually, Phil called me and told me what happened. He couldn't even look at Steve. I confirmed what Phil had told me with the other guys, and then I called Steve. I told him I was sorry, but that we couldn't have that kind of thing going on. He begged, "Oh man, I didn't mean it. Let me do your new band, Killing Machine." I was like, "Hell, no! You're going to hit me with a newspaper!" You know? (laughs). So we let him go, and that was that.

MT: From 1994 through early 1999, L.A. Guns stayed busy putting out four more albums, but experienced consistent personnel changes, even touring as a four-piece band for the first time. How did you like touring as a four-piece band?

TG: I always preferred playing as a four-piece, but didn't mind playing as a five-piece band because in the case of Izzy and Mick, they are such great rhythm guitar players. It's a *feel* thing that not everyone has. When I play with another guitar player, I always have to be thinking about what they are doing so that I don't run all over their playing. So when there is not another guy there, it makes it really easy for me to not have to think about anything else while I'm playing.

MT: During this period L.A. Guns had four different lead vocalists, including Ralph Saenz (Michael Starr) from Steel Panther. Why did he leave L.A. Guns?

TG: It was such a bummer! I was such good friends with him, and he was such a great singer in L.A. Guns. He's a sober guy. I think we had played a gig in Dallas, which was one of our last shows on that tour. He hooked up with some girl that had given him some valium or something. I remember walking up to the front of the bus, and Ralph was watching TV, but he was really goofy. He was like, "Hey man, what's *happening*?" I asked him if he was alright, and he said, "Yeah, I feel *great*." I knew something wasn't right. I remember we decided to walk to a Whataburger which was about two blocks away. He had his arm around me the entire time saying, "I love you so much, Bro" and I'm like, "Holy shit! What is wrong with this guy?" (laughs). So, we get home and a couple days later, he comes to my house. He sits on my couch and goes, "Dude, I can't go on tour anymore." I asked, "What are you talking about?" He says, "I totally fucked up my sobriety." I go, "You were fucked up that last week of the tour, weren't you?" He goes, "Yep." He did the right thing for himself, and I am really happy the way it turned out for him, but it was a real bummer for me. I really liked playing with him.

MT: In 1999 L.A Guns toured with Ratt, Great White, and Poison. Is it true that you joined Poison briefly, filling in for C.C. Deville?
TG: All of the guys in Poison had called me individually. I had known those guys since way back in the day, since day one practically. So yes, later in 1999 when C.C wanted to do his own thing, they called me. They said, "I know this might be weird." I said, "It's not weird. Will I have my own backstage?" (laughs). I said, "You're going to pay me a lot of money, and I'm going to have my own deli tray. Don't worry about the music - the guitar playing will be fine." And they laughed. We started rehearsing writing some new stuff, which was alright. But then we starting playing the old stuff, and that sounded really good. Then one day, they all called me again, and they said, "C.C. wants back in. We think it's the right thing to do." I'm like, "That's cool. Make sure you pay me." It was all cool. That was the closest I have ever come to having my own dressing room. (laughs).

MT: In April of 2001, L.A. Guns released the album, *Man in the Moon,* then released *Waking the Dead* in August of 2002. This was the last L.A. Guns album you would be featured on till 2011. Did you tell the band you were leaving?
TG: I never told them I was leaving. We were touring supporting *Waking the Dead.* We were out with a bunch of crap bands that I didn't want anything to do with. I was talked into doing that tour. This guy, Obi Steinman, called himself a manager, but was really out for himself. He made some really bad decisions on our behalf. Steve Riley went along with him, and they both convinced me to do this tour. Right before the tour, I had spoken with Nikki Sixx about doing a side project, which ended up being Brides of Destruction. So we were doing the photo shoot for *Waking the Dead*, and I told everybody that I was going to do the side project for at least one record, maybe two, with Nikki after the tour. I told the guys that after this project that we could get on a really good tour. It would be L.A. Guns opening for Motley Crue. Everybody was like, "That would be great! You gotta do it! blah, bablah, bablah." So we did the tour, and I was writing the Brides record

while on that tour. The band was talking a lot about Brides of Destruction, and all my guys are pretending to be really supportive of it. So, it was getting towards the end of the tour, and I asked everyone, "What do you guys want to do while I am working with Brides?" They said they didn't know. I said, "You should carry on. You guys need to make a living. Why don't you guys get another guitar player, and when everything happens it will happen, and we'll go do it." They were like, "Oh yeah, yeah, yeah. That's a great idea, we'll go do that." I didn't mean, "Here, take my band and do whatever the fuck you want with it!" (laughs).

MT: Your new venture, Brides of Destruction, featured you and Nikki Sixx from Motley Crue. Tell us about the first meeting with Nikki that started the ball rolling on the project.
TG: I had thought about this project for about six months before I put anything into motion. I talked with Taime from Faster Pussycat about it as I knew he was friends with Nikki. I hadn't seen Nikki in about 15 years. I pitched it to Taime with him being the singer with Nikki and I, and we would find a drummer. We would call the band, Devil. He thought it was a great idea, but I told him that he had to reach out to Nikki, because I didn't know how to get a hold of him. Of course, he never did. I had another mutual friend of Nikki's, and I asked her to have him contact me. The timing was right because Motley wasn't doing anything, and I had some free time as well. Nikki got back with me right away, within an hour. I told him my entire concept, and then I told him that I have great ideas but terrible follow through. So I said, "I'm going to give you this idea. Now I need you to follow through on it!" (laughs). Nikki was interested, but told me that he was currently discussing another project which was a very early Velvet Revolver. He said it could be fun to include me in that. I told Nikki, "That's cool. But I really want to do this Devil project, so if yours doesn't work out, let me know." I knew it wasn't going to work out because Slash is a player. He doesn't have patience. He wants the bass player to be fuckin' John Paul Jones *today*. Nikki wasn't at that level at that time. As a matter of fact, Nikki hadn't played bass in two years at that point. A day went by, and Nikki called me. He said, "Let's do this other thing. That Slash guy is hard to get close to." (laughs). Nikki is a pretty sensitive guy. I went over to his place and brought him some tunes. He picked up his bass, and couldn't play in time. He felt bad about it, but I told him to take his time and practice this week. And he did! The thing about Nikki is that he is a sponge. You can show the guy anything and he can play it. He spent a lot of time practicing on his own. I didn't

have to teach him, or instruct him on anything. The next thing I know he is showing up to rehearsal with a 5 string bass, and has turned into Super Bass Guy! But early on, we talked a lot. We talked a thousand more hours than we played. Nikki is a big picture guy. He wants the stage to look a certain way, and he's kind of strict. Here's a great example: One night, I didn't feel like putting on the monkey suit. I had my heels on, but with a pair of flared jeans. He asked me, "What are you doing?" I had no idea what he was talking about. "What's up with those pants?" I go, "I always wear these pants." He says, "Not on stage, you don't." (laughs). But I have to say, man. That band. Those were some of the highest points of my career.

MT: During this time, Phil Lewis and Steve Riley made a public announcement that they would continue in L.A. Guns without you. What were your initial thoughts?
TG: My initial thoughts were that all of the french fry makers and burger flippers just took over my business! But of course they did this after I learned that Steve had been taking our co-publishing checks and was cashing them, and keeping all of the money and not distributing it. That's why I would never play with those guys again. All this happened within the first four months that I was doing Brides. Steve knows that too. I will *never* play with him again. That's how things ended up the way they are at this point.

MT: Nikki Sixx left Brides of Destruction in 2004, and you worked on numerous projects until 2006 when you started The Tracii Guns Band, which would later become Tracii Guns, L.A. Guns. Will there continue to be two versions of L.A. Guns?
TG: It's really difficult *not* to do L.A. Guns when your name is Tracii Guns, you know? The one thing I will say is that we will not record any new music as L.A. Guns. We made our best records a long time ago. But to say that I am going to walk away from L.A. Guns, it's not even possible.

MT: You were recently critical of Steve Riley on "That Metal Show." Has your opinion of him changed since the shows taping?
TG: No, he is still a douche bag that belongs in jail.

MT: In 2011, your band released "Acoustic Gypsy Live" with Jizzy Pearl singing. Would you do an acoustic tour?
TG: I talked about that with one of my agents. His thought was that there are specific rooms that are ideal for acoustic performances. Many

of the smaller venues across the country don't have the capacity to have seven people sit on stage with a piano and do it properly. They are just not set up for that physically or sonically. We had also tossed around the idea of just doing 10 acoustic shows by popping into some of the larger cities. But, we never really got any legs to promote that record because Jizzy was out of the band even before the record came out. It just didn't make any sense. I talked to Steve Vai about it because he owns my label. He goes, "Look man, we already made all the money on it. Who cares? Let's move on to the next thing." I was like, "Alright, cool."

MT: Tell us about Tracii Guns, League of Gentlemen.
TG: This is what I have been trying to do my whole life. We are almost done with our record. I can't describe the record because it's indescribable. There is a blues song, a rock'n'roll song, a metal song, a folk song, and they are all played with the style of my earliest influences. Hank Williams-style to a Rolling Stones-style, Hendrix, Zeppelin - it's a classic rock band. The idea of the band is to walk on stage with a set of songs, and completely obliterate those songs. If we come to a point in a song and I don't feel like playing the next part, I have such chemistry with these guys that I can take the song wherever it needs to go, and they will follow me. This is what I did in the garage when I was 11 and 12 years old. We would just jam all day, and go back and forth between rockabilly and heavy metal. The League of Gentlemen is a forever evolving, or devolving, musical situation.

MT: Let me ask you some personal questions. How do you feel the last night of a long tour?
TG: Generally, I am happy.

MT: If you were asked to do MTV's Cribs, would you do it?
TG: Sure.

MT: How big is your current place you call home?
TG: Pretty big. (laughs). 2400 square feet, four bedrooms, two bathrooms. It's on a full acre in the Hollywood Hills.

MT: What kind of car(s) do you own?
TG: I have the mama mobile which is a Mercedes SUV, child-safe car. I have a '57 Chevy, a '48 Ford truck, a huge F-350 truck, I have an F-350 van. I have a lot of cars!

MT: Are you in a position that you never have to work again?
TG: No, I always have to work.

MT: Are you registered to vote?
TG: No.

MT: Do you smoke cigarettes? How many a day?
TG: I do. At home, about a pack a day. On tour, at least two packs a day.

MT: Where is your favorite local place to hang out?
TG: I'm kind of fond of the Bourgeois Pig.

West Springfield, Virginia. July 2009.
Photo: Robin Watts Photography.

MT: How often are you recognized in public?
TG: When I go out in public, I am recognized each time. They go, "Man, you're old!" (laughs).

MT: Who is the biggest douche in rock'n'roll?
TG: Let me think about this because I want to answer this one. Man, you know. I know it's going to bum him out, and maybe not currently, but at one time Bobby Blotzer was the biggest douche in rock'n'roll.

MT: What was your drug of choice back in the day?
TG: I never did drugs back in the day, but now its weed.

MT: If you took a drug test today, what would it tell us?
TG: That I smoke weed.

MT: Should marijuana be legalized?
TG: It should be for us, it shouldn't be for the growers. The growers make their money and their profits because they are able to do what they do illegally, and it works out better for the public. On the other hand, to legalize marijuana and charge $100 an ounce where 50% of that tax goes back into the local economy makes a lot of sense to me. So, I am for it and against it for different reasons.

MT: Do you follow sports?
TG: I follow the Lakers.

MT: Craziest groupie story?
TG: Seven girls and me in the back of a bus in 1988. It was awesome!

MT: Of all the clubs on the Sunset Strip, which is your favorite and why?
TG: I have to go with The Whisky, which is an odd choice. It's just The Whisky, man. They have good oxygen on stage.

MT: When was your last run in with the law?
TG: It was November in Atlanta. Dilana was singing in L.A. Guns at the time, and her and this guy got wasted together. We were staying at his house. This guy started going off on the other guys in the band, and I punched him in the face a couple times. They called the cops, and they almost got arrested, and we just left.

MT: Who do you listen to now?
TG: I listen to The Heavy a lot. It's an English band with a black singer. They play rock'n'roll. They have loops, and they are fuckin' insane! I also listen to Elton John, Otis Rush, and a lot of old blues, because I record and mix my own shit now. I listen to a lot of Hendrix and a lot of Zeppelin. A lot of stuff that was recorded in mono to help me get to where I need my stuff sounding.

MT: Do you have a pre-gig, warm up ritual?
TG: I usually have a shot or two of vodka before I play. I prefer to listen to music before I play, but it's not always possible. Basically, I walk out there, hit the volume pedal, and just go. I don't even warm up anymore.

MT: What beverage do you drink during a show?
TG: Coca Cola, or room temperature water. Beer just makes me want to puke when I am playing, but I'm not a real beer drinker. After the show, I always drink chocolate milk. It puts all of the sugar back in your body.

MT: Who is the one person that you run into knowing you're going to have a long night of partying ahead of you?
TG: Lemmy.

MT: When was the last time you were blown away by a band's live performance?
TG: Beitthemeans from Birmingham, Alabama. They are a three-piece. They are loud and mean.

MT: Who are the three best living rock guitarists?
TG: Jack White, Jimmy Page, and Jeff Beck.

MT: When you look back at your career, what gig do you have the fondest memory of?
TG: It's absolutely the Download Festival in 2004 with Brides of Destruction.

MT: 2013 will bring us to the 30th Anniversary of L.A. Guns. Are you planning anything big?
TG: No. (laughs). Plans are God's way of making him laugh.

Tracii at Blues Garage, Isernhagen, Germany. March 2012. Photo by Regine Lube

MT: What advice would you provide to a player who wants to play rock music for a living?

TG: If you go into playing rock 'n' roll thinking that you are going to make a living at it, you are a fool. My advice would be play rock 'n' roll because you love it, and if you happen to make a living out of it, you are in the $1/100^{th}$ of $1/100^{th}$ of a percent of people who try to make a living playing rock 'n' roll.

MT: What are you working on now?

TG: Right now, it's all about The League of Gentlemen, which you can check out at www.facebook.com/traciigunsband. The record is close to being done, so hopefully in time for Christmas 2012. If not, early 2013. We will be touring a lot, breaking in the new material and playing the L.A. Guns stuff as well.

Paul in Madrid Spain with VAS, October 2011.

Paul Shortino

Lead Vocals

Past-Rough Cutt, Quiet Riot

Present-King Kobra, VAS

MT: When is your birthday?
PS: May 14.

MT: Marital status?
PS: Married.

MT: Do you have any kids?
PS: One. I also have two grandkids.

MT: City you were born?
PS: Lima, Ohio.

MT: City you currently reside?
PS: Las Vegas, Nevada.

MT: Do you own or rent your home?
PS: We own our home.

MT: How many square feet is your home?
PS: The house is around 2500 square feet.

MT: How much is your mortgage payment?
PS: It's paid for.

MT: How old were you the first time you sang to an audience?
PS: I was five or six years old. My mom and dad had a bar, and my mom was a singer. We used to all go down and sing with my mom at the bar.

MT: When did you know that you wanted to make a living from singing?
PS: I was watching the Ed Sullivan Show and saw Elvis, The Beatles, and The Stones. The first song I learned on guitar was "House of the Rising Sun" after I saw the Animals on there. His show was like MTV back in the day. I had a total passion and love for it, then I found out you could get chicks playing music! (laughs)

MT: In 1971, you had a hit that made the charts?
PS: Yes! It was a song called, "Follow Me". It was recorded on Bell Records, and produced by Snuff Garrett. He had produced artists like Sonny & Cher and Liza Minnelli. We were called Paul & JoJo. It hit the charts at #22 with a bullet. I thought, "Wow! This is great!" Then all of the sudden Vicki Lawrence came out with "The Night the Lights Went Out in Georgia" on the same label, and my little 45 was shelved!

MT: Then in 1972, you had some trouble with the law?
PS: Yes. I was arrested for pot. I had just turned 18. I was at rehearsal, and was going to hang out with my dad that night, so I grabbed my coat when I left. We went and visited my uncle who had a few bars in Compton. I think we were the only white guys driving a Cadillac in the area. It was a prominently black neighborhood. The police pulled us over, and I was asked for my license. I checked my coat pocket but my wallet wasn't there. I then realized that I had grabbed one of the other guy's coats when I left rehearsal. When I told them that I didn't have my license, they started searching me. They ended up finding a small bag of weed in the jacket - it was hardly anything. So, I went to jail. I was the only white kid in there, and my dad begged them to give me my own cell because I was fresh meat at the Compton Jail. My record was on the charts at the time, and I thought that my career was over. I was licking my wounds in jail, and my dad ended up bailing me out after a couple days. Then I tried to keep my hind end out of trouble! (laughs)

MT: You were in various bands during the next few years, then in 1980, your friend, Dave Alford, introduced you to Ronnie James Dio. How did that go down?
PS: I had met Dave at a car wash. I told him I could sing, so we got together and I played him some stuff. At that time, I was in a band with Claude Schnell, who would eventually end up in Ronnie James Dio's band. Our band was called, Magic, at the time. Dave brought in a guitar player named Bob DeLellis. Then we brought in another

guitarist, Jake Williams, who ended up being Jake E. Lee. My step father had built a recording studio, and we did some demos there. We then went to the Record Plant with Eddie Delena, and did some demos there as well. Then, Ronnie James Dio came to a rehearsal one night, and after he heard us, he wanted to do something with the band. He said that he really loved my voice. The next thing you know, I was in litigation trying to get out of a contract with the guys that were previously managing me. Ronnie and Wendy Dio took me to their attorney, Stan Diamond, and he was the one who started the process of getting me out of my contract. That is how I met Ronnie and Wendy.

MT: How did you and Jake get a long?
PS: Jake was a piece of cake. We got along great for a long period of time. He had the opportunity to get into Ozzy. I didn't want to stop anybody from moving forward.

MT: Could you tell that Jake was destined for big things even back then?
PS: I think he wanted to be Ronnie's guitar player. There was a falling out somewhere, with Ronnie and him, but then the Ozzy opportunity popped up. We all knew that with his stage appearance and playing, that the gig was his. He was a star in his own right. We knew he would get the gig, and we wished him the best when he got it.

MT: About this time you were invited to audition for the part of 'Duke Fame' in the movie "This is Spinal Tap." Is it true that Jake was up for the part as well?
PS: We put out an ad with our picture in the paper. We were playing the Troubadour. The casting director for the movie saw the ad in the paper, saw the way we looked, and came down to our gig. He spoke with us and wanted Jake, Dave (Alford, drums), and I to come down to "Norm's" the next day for a potential part in the movie. I had on a white leather outfit with knee-high suede boots for the gig that night. Well, I showed up the next day in that same outfit, and I showed up there first! I got the part because of the way I was dressed, and because I showed up at the casting call. The wardrobe lady said, "We don't even need to dress him!" (laughs)

MT: You must have had some laughs filming your scene?
PS: Oh, man! When we got to the set at the Burbank Holiday Inn, I was able to watch the guys do a few of their scenes. I didn't really know the guys who were part of the band, but I remember leaning over

to Wendy Dio and saying, "These guys are having a really bad hair day." So everyone breaks for lunch, and we are all sitting at this round table. Wendy is to my right, Rob Reiner to my left. I was talking to everyone at the table about helping them with the music if they needed some songs. I was informed that they had their own material, but all of it was cheesy-type stuff. I was just trying to get some music in a movie, you know? So I look to the guys sitting across the table from us and say, "You know, you look like those guys who are having a really bad hair day!" They didn't have their wigs on! (laughs) One of the guys says, "We are! Hi, I am Michael McKean." (laughs) That part in the movie got me my SAG card. Actually, doing that part got Rough Cutt sound checks once the movie came out! We were playing in front of Accept and Krokus on tour. At the time, we weren't getting a line check or anything before we went on. The road manager for Krokus comes by our dressing room one night and says, "Aren't you Duke Fame?" I told him that I was. He asked me to come back to Krokus's dressing room because the guys wanted to meet me. I go back there, sign autographs as Duke Fame, and all of a sudden, we start getting a line check! (laughs)

MT: Do you remember what you got paid for that gig?
PS: It was around $1200.

MT: Prior to Rough Cutt being managed by Wendy Dio, you moved in with the Dio's?
PS: Yes. When they were trying to get me out of my contract, they thought I was such a trustworthy kind of guy who would believe anything that anybody told me. That's how I got in the contract mess in the first place. They said, "We're going to move you into the house because we are afraid that you will sign anything!" (laughs) I lived with them for two and a half years.

MT: What was it like to live with Ronnie James Dio?
PS: It was awesome! It was awesome just to be around him. I would have Thanksgiving at the Dio's house, and I'm meeting Mark Stein from Vanilla Fudge, Glenn Hughes from Deep Purple. I am meeting people that I would have never met. Sometimes I would make English muffins and tea for them when they got up. I would try to be invisible, you know, because they took me in their home. At times I would sit up with Ronnie during all hours of the night. We became close, like brothers. It was quite an experience.

MT: Did you spend a lot of time in the studio with Ronnie?

PS: Oh, yeah. I remember that Wendy was managing Ronnie and Rough Cutt at the time, and she thought that Ronnie was making me sound a little bit too much like him. So, I am in the studio with Ronnie, and we're cutting this track. And he is making me sing like…well, a little like Ronnie! I found out just recently after talking to Angelo, his engineer, that Ronnie was really heartbroken when he and Angelo didn't get to produce the Rough Cutt record. We were signed to Warner Bros, and we waited a year for Ted Templemen to produce the album, but that never happened. I think if Ronnie would have produced the album, it would have been rougher and rawer, and sounded less produced. And it would have come out before Ratt, Dokken, and all of the other bands that beat us to the punch while we were waiting for Ted.

MT: Some changes were made to Rough Cutt's line-up in 1984, and then you went on tour with Dio. Was that a difficult gig, opening for RJD?

PS: We were very well accepted by the crowds. It was more difficult working with the reps for Warner Bros, not so much opening for Ronnie. Timing is everything. We were on the largest grossing tour in America at the time, opening for Dio on their Sacred Heart Tour. You couldn't even find our albums in record stores!

MT: Did you hang with the Dio guys, post-show? Who was the biggest partier in that group?

PS: (laughs) Jimmy Bain. We got to hang with everyone, but one thing was really bad. Vinny (Appice) had flying bass drums on his drum kit. So our drummer, Dave Alford, decided that he was going to have some flying tom toms on his kit. They almost had the same set up. When you're out on the road, you learn tricks from people. You use a few of them while you're out with someone, but you don't steal everything. David started copying parts of Vinny's drum solo and using it in his. Now, we are warming up for them. You don't do that. That is a no-no.

MT: Did Vinny get upset by that?

PS: Oh, hell yeah he did! It drew a little line in the sand there. Also, anytime Ronnie had something going on, whether it was press or anything, Wendy pushed us in there, whether we wanted to be or not. So, there was a *little* bit of animosity between certain people in our band. Because basically, we were riding on Ronnie's coat tails. It didn't matter that we were signed to Warner Bros. He could have had anybody warm up for him on that tour. I will say, though, that Ronnie always gave us full sound. Most headliners will hold back some of the volume during the opening band, but Ronnie never did that.

MT: Vivian Campbell was only 20 years old at the time. What was he like?
PS: Vivian was a very shy quiet guy. A humble gentleman.

MT: During this time Ronnie assembled the largest group of top shelf Heavy Metal talent ever for the Hear 'n Aid project. How cool was that?
PS: That was the probably the coolest event that I have ever been at. I don't know where I was when they took the main photo of everybody, but I am not in that photo. I must have gone to the bathroom. I don't think the publicist realized that I wasn't in the photo when she picked that photo for the cover.

MT: Was there a buffet of drugs and booze during recording?
PS: Ronnie and Wendy were very down on drugs. But, pot was okay. Ronnie was a pothead. I am a pothead. But, no, I didn't see any drugs going on. If there were any, it was behind closed doors because Ronnie was so down on heroin, coke, and drugs like that.

MT: Were there any in the group who didn't get along?
PS: No. That was the most incredible gathering of egos that I have ever been at, but everyone was so humble about what was going on. We were all just there to do our parts.

MT: Who was the biggest partier in that group?
PS: Jimmy Bain and I got pretty wasted. He liked to drink Jim Beam and coke, so did I, and so did Ronnie. When we went in the studio to cut vocals, that's what we were drinking. We used to call Jimmy Bain, Jimmy Beam! (laughs)

MT: Did you hang out much with Kevin Dubrow during the recording?
PS: Oh, Kevin and I were very good friends, even before that.

MT: Tell us a funny story from those couple days.
PS: The funniest story was that me, Neil Schon, and Geoff Tate were in our hospitality suite after we recorded that day. It was at the top of

the Holiday Inn that we were staying at. In walks Rob Halford with his boyfriend. Nobody knew he was gay at the time. I never thought he was, but it doesn't matter. The guy sings his ass off. Rob's room ended up being right next to the hospitality suite, and later that night there were some crazy, wild noises coming out of his room. We were kind of chuckling saying, "I think Rob is in there with his boyfriend!"

MT: In 1987, you left Rough Cutt, and within a year you had replaced Kevin Dubrow in Quiet Riot. How did that all happen?
PS: I had been buddies with Kevin, and met Frankie and Carlos through the Hear 'n Aid thing. Shortly after that, Rough Cutt was touring Japan in support of their second album, and Quiet Riot was touring Japan supporting their third album. The two bands got along very well, and we had listened to each other's albums when we would hang out. We were all friends, and I think that the guys in Quiet Riot liked me as a person and they liked my voice. So here we are touring Japan, and Kevin and his band part ways. Rough Cutt gets dropped from our label. At this time we were having musical differences, but we were hanging in there. We come home, and Wendy hears that Quiet Riot is looking for a singer. She told me to check it out, and that it would be good for my career. I asked her, "What about the band?" Rough Cutt was in the studio re-recording songs trying to get another deal. I also learned that Quiet Riot only had one more album on their contract with CBS/Sony/PASHA records. So they called me, and I go down to PASHA Studios to meet with Frankie and Carlos. We all got along well during the meeting, and I joined the band.

MT: Once you joined Quiet Riot, did you get along with your band mates?
PS: We got along great until the managers had to sign their management deal. They went from 20% to 15%, and they had to split the management with Wendy Dio because she was my manager. There was so many politics in Quiet Riot that it really soured the band. Later when the managers, Warren Entner and Wendy, sat down to work things out, Warren told Wendy that he didn't want her involved in anything. She told him that she would take her client and find me my own solo deal then. Warren ran back to Frankie and Carlos and told them that I was just in Quiet Riot to land a solo gig. So then, no one would talk to anybody. It was two weeks before we were to shoot a video, and no one is talking. We all finally got together to work it out, but everything went from "Bros" to "Business". Music people should do music, and business people should do business. When you get music

people and business people together, it usually hurts everything. This really kind of hurt our relationship.

MT: Rumor has it that Frankie and Carlos weren't getting along well during this time?
PS: I don't think that they have ever gotten along. I don't know why they didn't get along, but I just know that I was the outcast. Ever since Warren had told the other guys that I was just in it for the solo deal. This is after I had worked all year with them writing close to 90% of the material, and giving it up as the publishing was split equally.

MT: Did you ever visit with Kevin after you joined Quiet Riot?
PS: Oh, yeah. We were buds. We would hang out together.

MT: Tell us about the choreographer you hired?
PS: I was working out with a personal trainer, and I was hitting the gym hard. I was on an all-protein diet. I was trying to lose weight and get in shape. I also hired Serge, who was a choreographer for "Cats". I told him that I didn't want any gay kind of stuff, I wanted to look cool, so yeah, I was taking private lessons. I even borrowed money from my little brother, Vinny, to help pay for some of the things to get me bulked up.

MT: How was the publishing split with Quiet Riot?
PS: It was supposed to be equal, but Spencer (Proffer) ended up getting more. But the band split their portion equally.

MT: After Quite Riot, you did an album with Jeff Northrup, and then formed Badd Boyz with Mitch Perry and Sean McNabb. Rumor has it that Mitch liked to cocktail?
PS: Oh yeah. Mitch was a party animal!

MT: Around this time, is it true that Carmine Appice asked you to join him and John Sykes in Blue Murder?
PS: Yes, they asked me to audition. They also auditioned Jeff Scott Soto and Derek St. Holmes. What's funny is John Sykes ended up singing the stuff himself, and did a phenomenal job with it. I don't even know why they were looking for a vocalist.

MT: You sang on nearly 10 tribute albums during 1997-2002. Do you have a favorite tribute album experience?

PS: I really liked *Dragon Attack*. That was a tribute to Queen. I did the vocals on "We Will Rock You".

MT: Jumping ahead to 2010, you joined Carmine Appice's band, King Kobra. How has that experience been?
PS: It's been awesome! We got great reviews on our latest record, and we are going to be doing another one. I also did another record with Carmine and Javier Vargas on Warner Bros. We toured Spain last year.

MT: You have played with some amazing guitar players. Who would you classify as the best you have played with?
PS: Wow. Well, Jeff Northrup is a very talented songwriter and so is David Henzerling from King Kobra. Both of those guys are very talented song writers and guitar players. Jake is a great guitar player, but we didn't experience the song writing magic that I have experienced with Jeff and David. Also, Javier Vargas is another one. He is a very tasteful, bluesy-type of guitar player.

MT: And drummers?
PS: Carmine is the best drummer that I have ever played with.

MT: You and Ronnie James Dio became good friends. What is your fondest memory of him?
PS: Sitting up watching "Fawlty Towers" at his house. Just hanging out and being friends. Working in the yard! (laughs) Actually, the fondest memories I have of Ronnie is hanging in the studio. Because music is something we both really loved, and that was probably the most exciting time.

MT: You performed at his Memorial Service. Was that a difficult performance?
PS: Yeah. And I chose a song that wasn't a Dio song. I did John Lennon's, "In My Life". From one great legend to another, you know? Everybody had picked all of the great songs that I wanted to do, so I went ahead and picked a song that wasn't his song, but pretty much said what life is about. It was tough. I actually poured my heart out there. A lot of people came up to me afterward and told me that they didn't actually break til I broke down. When I started the song, I told everyone that I didn't know if I could get through it. I kind of think that I broke the ice, where they saw the real Paul and they felt comfortable letting their own feelings out.

MT: Do you have a pre-gig ritual?
PS: I just ask God to let me have a good show. I really don't warm up.

MT: What kind of car do you drive?
PS: We have a couple cars. I have a 2002 PT Cruiser with the seats out in the back, and doggie beds. That is the doggie car. It's paid for. I also have a 2010 Cadillac STS, 4-door. That's the wife's car. It's paid for as well.

MT: Do you smoke cigarettes?
PS: No. I haven't smoked cigarettes in 14 years.

MT: What was your drug of choice back in the day?
PS: Coke.

MT: If you took a drug test today, what would it tell us?
PS: That I smoke weed.

MT: Should marijuana be legalized?
PS: Absolutely. With restrictions, of course.

MT: How is your health?
PS: I am in the best health I have ever been in. I would attribute that to good food, good sex, a good marriage, and no substance. I don't drink hard liquor anymore.

Paul and Carmen Shortino, Las Vegas Nevada. May 2012.

MT: What is your cocktail of choice?
PS: Good wine. White or Red.

MT: Are you registered to vote? Who will you vote for in 2012?
PS: Oh, yeah. It won't be President Obama. (laughs) I am actually an independent, or Libertarian. I believe in the constitution, and I would love to see Ron Paul get the nomination, but I don't think that will happen. I just don't believe in Obamanomics. I don't understand why a lot of people in the entertainment industry and the media are so on-board for him to take their money that they worked hard for, and spread it around.

MT: Have you ever toured Canada in the winter? Do you have any good stories there?
PS: I have, and I do! We stopped off at this gas station in the middle of nowhere to refuel the bus, and I had to use the restroom. I had gotten off the tour bus in a pair of slippers, my tank top, and sweat pants. This was way in the Northeast part of Canada, way above Quebec, and it was snowing like crazy. The men's head was disgusting, so I went into the ladies room. I sat down on the john to take a nice number two, and I hear something like a plane taking off. Of course, it was the bus. I guess they checked the men's head and when they didn't see me in there, they assumed I had gotten back on the bus and took off! I jumped up, and started running down the road after them. As I was running, I would turn around to check for cars, and it was snowing so hard that my tracks in the snow were being covered as soon as I would leave them! Thank god they had stopped about two and a half miles down the road to get something to eat, and I caught up with them. If they hadn't stopped, I would still be chasing them.

MT: If you could write your own ticket and sing for any existing band, who would it be?
PS: Foreigner has always been one of my favorites. I will say, though, that Kelly Hanson is doing a phenomenal job. Also, Bad Company because I love Paul Rogers.

MT: Have you ever been afraid for your safety while on stage performing?
PS: Yes, it was in Pereira, Columbia. This was with Quiet Riot. We were playing in this soccer stadium, and we went on before the warm-up band. There were still people half way around the soccer stadium outside trying to get in. So when we quit playing, they rioted. They stared throwing shit at us. We had this big fence in front of us, like chicken wire and stuff, but we were actually hiding behind the amps as

people were rioting and trying to climb the fence. Our lighting guy was at the top of the stadium filming people around the stadium trying to get in, and he was narrating what was going on. I still have that footage. Also, while we were down there, their government said that our crew needed visas, which they didn't. But they ended up putting our whole crew in jail. That's when I decided to buy a $50 ball of cocaine the size of a softball. We had a big coffee table in the bar area of our suite. It was an incredible suite on the 31st floor of the Hilton in Bogota. And since we couldn't get out of the country, I bought a softball of cocaine. It was the most incredible coke that you would ever want to try. The coffee table had the image of a world map on it, so we were doing lines from Bogota to France, France to Florida, Florida to Moscow. I think that ball must have been a couple ounces.

MT: If you had a crystal ball, what age would it tell us you live to?
PS: My grandfather lived until he was 91, and he worked very hard his whole life. The shape that I'm in, I would bet I make 100.

MT: Should Quiet Riot be in The Rock and Roll Hall of Fame?
PS: I think that some of the other people who were big in the 80's, like Ronnie James Dio, should go before Quiet Riot.

MT: While on tour, have you ever called a city by the wrong name?
PS: You know, I think so. I don't remember the exact city, but when I saw that, "Wanna Get Away?" commercial from Southwest Airlines, it really hit a nerve!

MT: Who is the funniest band mate you had to share a hotel room with on tour?
PS: Jimmy Waldo when I was in Quiet Riot, and Matt Thorne from Rough Cutt. Matt used to bring girls back to the room, and after he would have his way with them, he would tell them to get a Coke. The girls would run out to get the Coke, and he would put their clothes out in the hallway and lock them out. (laughs)

MT: When you sing in the car or shower, is it typically your songs that you sing?
PS: No. I only sing my stuff in the car or shower when I am preparing to go on the road, and have to remember stuff. You know, a lot of times I prefer singing R&B stuff around the house or in the car. I am an R&B singer that got stuck in the heavy metal thing because it was a door to get a deal. I love R&B stuff.

MT: What advice would you provide to a vocalist who wants to play rock music for a living?

PS: Learn how to read and write music. Get professional training. Don't just jump out there. I did. I just jumped out there without any professional training at first, and I wish that I wouldn't have. Early on, my voice would be very raspy after I sang for three or four nights in a row because I was singing wrong. That is when I got professional training.

MT: What are you working on now? How can people get a hold of you?

PS: You can go to www.paulshortino.com or my Facebook fan page for current updates. You can also check out King Kobra's fan page on Facebook. We will start recording the new King Kobra album in June. I'm not sure if we will be doing a lot of touring with King Kobra, but I think we might do a few festivals. You can see our video and get other information about VAS at www.vargasblues.com. We'll start recording the new Vargas album on Warner Bros. in September of this year. VAS should be doing a good amount of touring to support it.

Paul and Carmine Appice performing with VAS in Munich, Germany. March 2012.

Chris performing at the House of Blues, Hollywood.
December 2011.

Chris Holmes

Lead Guitar

Past-W.A.S.P.

Present-W.A.S., Scum

MT: When is your birthdate?
CH: June 23, 1958.

MT: Where were you raised?
CH: La Canada Flintridge, California.

MT: Where do you currently reside?
CH: La Canada Flintridge, California.

MT: Did you graduate from high school?
CH: Yes. 1976.

MT: You told me earlier that you have a 4th grade reading level. Is that true?
CH: Well, it's around there. A doctor told me about four years ago that I have dyslexia. It kind of hampers you when learning stuff. I have never read a book in my life.

MT: Do you currently rent or own your home?
CH: Rent.

MT: How big is your place?
CH: (laughs) Oh, it's about 10 feet by 12 feet. (laughs again).

MT: What do you pay for rent?
CH: Zero. A friend I have known all my life lets me live there. It's a tool room behind a garage. This way when I go on the road, I can just lock it up and go.

MT: Marital status? Kids?
CH: Divorced, no kids. I have trouble enough taking care of myself!

MT: When did you pick up your first guitar?
CH: I was thirteen. My sister had an acoustic guitar; it was a flamenco catgut. I put some super slinkies on it. It bent the hell out of the neck, but it was perfect.

MT: Were you one of the cooler kids in high school due to being a guitar player?
CH: Not really. I was more or less a drughead in high school.

MT: What kind of drugs did you do in High School?
CH: You name it. Whatever was around. Back then it wasn't, "Say no to drugs." If you didn't do drugs, you were an outcast.

MT: When did you realize that you wanted to play music for a living?
CH: I was about thirteen. I saw the movie, "Jimi Hendrix."

MT: Have you ever auditioned for a band and not gotten the gig?
CH: Oh, tons of them. In 1979, I auditioned for Ozzy Osbourne the same night Randy Rhoads did. I played for Ozzy an hour and a half before he went to see Quiet Riot play.

MT: Where did your audition take place for Ozzy?
CH: In a studio off Lookout Mountain in Laurel Canyon.

MT: Who was there for the audition?
CH: Just Ozzy and Dana Strum.

MT: Who else have you auditioned for?
CH: I never played for them, but I sent some stuff off to UFO. I didn't get that gig. Probably because I was American, or horrible. I don't know. Another was a band called Stormer. I didn't get that one. I auditioned for L.A. Guns and got the gig, but that didn't last long. (laughs).

MT: What happened?
CH: L.A. Guns was set to tour Europe opening for Alice Cooper, but Tracii Guns was supposed to be in the band, and he wasn't at the time. Word leaked and when the promoter learned that Tracii wasn't going to

make the trip to Europe, they had to cancel the tour. It was actually a breach of contract touring without Tracii in the band. I just played a few local shows with them, and that was it.

MT: Around 1979, you joined the band "Sister" with Blackie Goozman. What kind of music did Sister play?
CH: It was hard rock, like Alice Cooper

MT: Sister disbanded months after you joined the band. Years later, Blackie formed the first version of W.A.S.P. You joined W.A.S.P. months later. Put the controversy to rest. Where did the name W.A.S.P. come from? What does it stand for?
CH: It came from the movie, "Road Warrior." We purposely used all capital letters with periods behind each one. This way if ten bands were mentioned one after another in print, we would stand out. Then someone said, "It must stand for something because of the periods." It could mean anything. "We Are Stupid Pricks?" But it really has no meaning.

MT: Early W.A.S.P. was known for their theatrics. Who was responsible for bringing the raw meat to the gig?
CH: Throwing the raw meat into the audience was Blackie's and my idea, mostly his. We did that as a way of touching the audience without having to actually go into the audience. The road crew was responsible for bringing the meat to the gig. We had more guys in the road crew than we did in the band, even early on.

MT: During these shows, you would put Hershey bars in your underwear?
CH: (laughs) It was peanut butter. I had the back of my pants cut out and I put peanut butter back there to make it look like crap. (laughs).

MT: Blackie would drink blood at each show. What was his "blood" made of?
CH: It was just stage blood. The stuff you would buy at Cinema Secrets.

MT: After W.A.S.P.'s first album came out, the PMRC (Parents Music Resources Center) and Tipper Gore came down hard on the band. What were the bands discussions like regarding the PMRC?
CH: We thought they were idiots. It was just the one song. Who are they to tell you what you can put on a record? It's freedom of speech, right?

MT: Is it true that venues you were scheduled to play would receive bomb threats, and that Blackie was actually shot at twice?
CH: I don't know about twice, but I remember we were doing a photo shoot at Trashy Lingerie on La Cienega. It was about midnight, and someone came by and stuck their head out the top of a moon roof and took some photos of us. One of our roadies went over and grabbed their camera. The car took off, but they came back moments later and just started shooting at us.

MT: What did you do?
CH: I hit the ground. They missed us, but broke the store windows.

MT: And the bomb threats?
CH: In Ireland, and a few other countries. We would still play though.

MT: Were you ever afraid for your safety while performing?

CH: In Europe, sometimes they would super glue razorblades to coins and throw them. I didn't like that. You go out to do a show and kick ass. No one really wants to do anything to you, but there were some threats in the Bible Belt when we went down there the first time.

MT: In 1986, Randy Piper left W.A.S.P. and Johnny Rod joined the band playing bass. Blackie switched to rhythm guitar. Did you prefer this arrangement as you now played all guitar leads?

Chris with W.A.S.P. circa 1988.

CH: I liked Randy a lot. We're still friends today. I liked having Randy in the band because it gave us some variety. I would always play as fast as I could, and Randy was more like Billy Gibbons. You know, the first show we ever did Blackie played guitar and Don Costa played bass. We got Tony (Richards, Drums) and Don from Dante Fox, which is now Great White. Our first show, Don put a cheese grater on his amp and was rubbing his knuckles on it bleeding all over the place. He played with a pick axe that you would mountain climb with. We did the one show, then the next time we rehearsed I went up to him and said, "Don, you are one of the best bass players that I have ever played with, but if you ever play out of tune with me on stage I'm going to chew your cock off in front of everybody and spit it in your face." He quit that night, and I got blamed for it. Don had auditioned for Ozzy and got the gig, but didn't know how to tell us, so that was his way out. Blackie blamed me for it. We had a showcase coming up, so Blackie said that he would play bass and bring Randy in to play guitar.

MT: Rumor has it that Blackie would fine you if you didn't play your guitar leads just right?
CH: Yes, he did.

MT: How much was the fine?
CH: $500. He fined me anytime I would screw up. It would keep me in line playing the same melodies. When I learned guitar, I didn't learn it from a book, because I couldn't read and I didn't go to any school. I learned it by ear. So when you play, you learn to jam, like blues. Improvisation. So, I would play what I felt, and he would get mad at me. There was also a time when I would get fined if I jumped into the audience. I remember in Ireland they would spit on you. When a kid spit on me, I dove right in after him.

MT: What would you do when you caught him?
CH: Smash his face in! You can strangle my dog, or kill my mom, but don't spit on me! Sometimes I would fill a squirt gun with piss, and squirt them in the face. That way I wouldn't have to go in the audience. I would do that a lot. They wouldn't even know that it was piss. Then I started using ammonia. They could really feel that, but the problem with the ammonia was that by the next day it would melt the squirt gun.

MT: Several years and successful albums later, Penelope Spheeris approached you to appear in her documentary, "Decline of Western Civilization II." Walk us through how it happened.
CH: We had a mutual friend, John Neff. I had seen Decline I, and she called me when I was in London while on a promo tour. She told me she was doing Decline II. I said, "Man, I hope it's not going to be as bad as the first one." She asked me to do an interview, and I told her to check with Blackie. She said she had just got off the phone with him. She didn't have the budget to do what he wanted to do, so that was cancelled. I told her that I would do the interview, and that I would be home next week.

MT: Was the pool scene filmed at your house at the time?
CH: No. It was at Miles Copeland's house. His brother is the drummer for The Police. Miles is the guy who dumped the money into the movie.

MT: In your infamous scene, you dump two bottles of vodka into your mouth and over your face while floating in a pool. Was that real booze? It seems like it should have burned your eyes?
CH: Yes, it was real. It did burn my eyes, if you go back and look at it.

MT: In hindsight, should you have taken a different approach to that scene?
CH: You know, kids come up to me sometimes and say that is the coolest thing they have seen in rock'n'roll. They look up to it. To me, it's kind of like starting at zero going down (laughs), but I used to drink like that. I never drank when I played, but after the gig, don't tell me what I can't do.

MT: Do you think it hurt your career?
CH: It put a huge damper on my trying to find work in other bands. People think that I am like that constantly. Who would want to work with someone like that? I guess I was needed in W.A.S.P. pretty damn bad! (laughs).

MT: What did you get paid for appearing in that scene?
CH: I never got paid. I was supposed to get $300, but I never did.

MT: About this time you had started dating Lita Ford, and eventually married her briefly. How cool was that?

CH: It was great. I can't say anything bad about her because there is nothing bad to say. She is great. I had a good marriage with her. When it was all said and done, I am surprised she hung around with me for that long.

MT: How was she as a lover?
CH: She was great. Oh, yeah.

MT: Why did you guys end up getting divorced?
CH: Because of my drinking. I was married once before Lita, and my first wife said, "If you don't stop drinking, I'm leaving." I said, "There's the door."

MT: What would Lita say if I asked her about you?
CH: Well (long pause), I couldn't tell you. She could say the worst thing in the world and it ain't going to make me look any worse (laughs). After Decline and all of the crap that is always said about me…(laughs).

MT: In 1989 you left W.A.S.P. for seven years. What did you do during that time?
CH: Oh, man. I kind of became a bum. I didn't have too much money. I played guitar with a few friends. I had a band called Psycho Squad. We all got along great, but we were all alcoholics. After that, I kind of lived on the streets in Hollywood. I was pretty down and out, but it was pretty fun. Some of the coolest people are on the streets. I don't know about trustworthy. It makes you humble when you climb up the ladder a little bit.

MT: You rejoined the band in 1996. How was your relationship with Blackie at this time?
CH: In 1988, we were very good friends. Then later that year, Lita was nominated for Vocalist of the Year. He made sure I couldn't go to the awards show. Ever since that night, if I had a life preserver in my hand and he fell off of the boat, I would not throw it to him. It wasn't right what he did.

MT: Why wouldn't he let you go?
CH: I didn't know the answer to that till 2001. I had called him an asshole. He asked why I called him an asshole. I said, "Why would you not let a so-called friend go to the Music Awards to support his wife?" He got up and as he walked out of the room he mumbled, "I was

jealous." My jaw hit the ground, man. That was the last time I ever spoke to him. Lita used to always tell me how jealous of me he was. I never saw it.

MT: How did the writing process work in W.A.S.P.?
CH: If you want to see the writing that I put into it, go to YouTube and search, "Circus Circus Love Machine." In the early days, the band was called Circus Circus. The video will be of Randy and Blackie. I joined the band six months after that video was shot. Then listen to Love Machine by W.A.S.P. The difference between the two is my contribution.

With W.A.S.P. circa 1984

MT: Were the publishing credits split 25% across the board in W.A.S.P.?
CH: I have not received a penny of publishing from W.A.S.P. through today. I was very young at the time, and the way my contract was written, any publishing that I was entitled to went right back into the band. I didn't know what I was doing, so I asked Blackie if I was doing the right thing in signing the contract the way it was written, and he said, "Yeah." I trusted him at the time. I was doing the right thing for him.

MT: So basically, you were just paid a flat salary to play in W.A.S.P.?
CH: Yes.

MT: Can I ask how much that was?
CH: In the early days it was $110 a week. When I left the band the first time in 1989, I was making $500 a week. When I came back in 1995, I got $1,000 a week before taxes.

MT: Looking at the publishing credits, it looks like Blackie wrote 80% of W.A.S.P.'s music. Does that sound right?
CH: No. The question should be, "How much did he steal?" 100%! He wrote most of the lyrics, but a lot of the stuff that he wrote was found in books.

MT: Let's take the song, "Wild Child." You received publishing on that, but didn't receive a penny?
CH: No. I never saw a penny on anything.

MT: It's interesting that he gave you any publishing credit at all.
CH: He had to. It would look kind of shitty if it were all him. The way he split it up was 33/33/33. Thirty-three for the lyrics, thirty-three for the melody of the lyrics, and thirty-three for the melody of the music. So, no matter what, the most I could get is thirty-three. And to top that off, I was never part of the meetings after the records were done to discuss who wrote what.

MT: So, who wrote the guitar riffs?
CH: I did. I wrote most of the riffs. I know that I wrote riffs on every song. There are probably 35-40 songs that I wrote the riff to and wasn't credited for the publishing.

MT: It's no wonder you are so fond of him!
CH: I thought we were friends at one time, but it's that jealousy. Being jealous of someone can be worse than being prejudice against them. I'm not jealous of any of my friends. Eddie Van Halen is a friend of mine, I'm not jealous the way he plays. I think it's bitchin'.

MT: W.A.S.P. toured with many different bands. Was there one band that you particularly liked?
CH: Iron Maiden. When we toured with them I would stay on Steve Harris's bus. They loved me because I was from here in Hollywood. (laughs). They are great people. Wouldn't you rather travel on their bus? (laughs).

MT: Was there one band that you didn't care for?
CH: I'd have to say Slayer. At the end of their show they would light lighters, and tell the kids to burn the hall down. They would yell, "Tear it down!" Man, you can't incite kids to start riots. It's probably just what they're all about, but it's kind of cold in a way.

MT: How much would you get for food per diem when touring with W.A.S.P.?
CH: In the early days, we got $200 a week. But when I came back, we didn't get anything. It was all coming out of the boss's pocket, you know?

MT: When is the last time you spoke to Blackie?
CH: That night we talked about earlier in 2001…I continued the tour, but we never spoke again.

MT: What would happen if Blackie called you today and asked you to rejoin the band?
CH: I would tell him to fuck off. After the things he's done, I don't know that the wound could ever be healed. I don't think that I could ever get the hatred I have for him out of my system.

MT: Everyone has their price. What would yours be?
CH: When I came back in '95, he asked me, "What will it take to keep you in the band?" I told him that I just wanted to be treated like a human being. A million dollar offer? I'd consider it, but you can't put a price on happiness.

MT: Would you say your guitar playing is better now than it has ever has been?
CH: The fire is still the same. I just play a lot slower. I would rather play one good note than play fifty thousand fast ones. I say that, and I still do the same old crap. I don't know why. It's not crap, it's just the way I play. Nick Bowcott (Grim Reaper) asked me what defines the chords that I play from anybody else, and we figured it out. It's stupid. I only hit two-note chords. I have never hit a three-note chord.

MT: You have said that you have taken a "state-paid vacation" for a while. Can you elaborate on that?
CH: A while back in 1981, I got my fifth DUI and the judge sent me up north to Vacaville for nine months. It's like a mental institution. I was locked up.

MT: Did you get anything out of it?
CH: (laughs) I still came out and drank and drive, so I guess I didn't.

MT: How much of your current income is from music?
CH: None of it.

MT: How do you make ends meet?
CH: I work for Larry Flynt. I work on pornos. I do the lights and the audio. I am a grunt guy. I don't mind the work and the people are really cool.

MT: Do you ever get to date the female talent?
CH: No. They work for an agency and are driven to the set. They get their hair and makeup done, they're told who they're going to suck, do their thing, and leave. They're cool.

MT: What does a gig like that pay?
CH: I make $500 for two days work.

MT: Have you ever collected unemployment?
CH: Yeah, I collected it against W.A.S.P. We were off the road and Blackie wouldn't even give me a retainer. Then back in 1982, I was about to go to jail for the DUIs, and I asked my boss to lay me off so that I could receive unemployment in jail. (laughs).

MT: What type of car do you drive?
CH: A 1987 Pontiac Trans Am. The engine runs, but the inside is gutted. It has no back seat. I have probably put nine transmissions in it. It's trashed, but I like it. I can move the seat back two feet and sit in the car comfortably. I'm going to try to auction the car off with Eddie Trunk's help.

MT: Over the years, did you have a favorite car that you owned?
CH: I had a '57 Chevy short bed, step side truck. I put a V8 in it. I used to drive that like a Wildman.

MT: Are you registered to vote?
CH: No.

MT: If it were a simple process would you have any of your tattoos removed?
CH: No.

MT: Who is the best musician you ever played with?
CH: I jammed with Tony Iommi (Black Sabbath) in his hotel room.
I've jammed with Eddie Van Halen at my house without drums and
bass. I had a house in Pasadena and he would come over. We'd smoke
a little ganja and get high. It was kind of funny because I had this
Marshall amp. He would play my guitar, and I would crank it up real
loud hoping that my neighbors would hear it, and think it was me!
(laughs).

MT: Do you smoke cigarettes? How many a day?
CH: I smoke about a pack a day of Camel Wides.

MT: Who is the biggest A-hole in rock'n'roll?
CH: Gene Simmons. Look at his TV show. I could also say Blackie
Lawless.

MT: What was your drug of choice back in the day?
CH: Cocaine.

**MT: How much money do you think you have spent on drugs in
your life?**
CH: Oh, man! (laughs). I have probably spent a half a million dollars.
(laughs).

MT: If you took a drug test today, what would it tell us?
CH: It would probably have a little bit of meth in it, and some
cannabis.

MT: Do you drink at all?
CH: No. I stopped February 5, 1996. I went to the Schick Center the
next day.

MT: How is your health?
CH: I don't know. The only time I see a doctor is in the emergency
room. I'm 53. I still act like a 14 year-old.

MT: When was the last time you made an emergency room visit?
CH: I went to Cedars Sinai once. I got stabbed. The knife almost went
through my temple. This was '93. I had got in a beef with one of the
18th Street gang members, and got the short end of the stick. I lost!
(laughs). There was about four or five of them, but I didn't give a shit. I
was hammered drunk.

MT: Have you been to Rehab? How many times?

CH: I have been to the Schick Center for Alcohol once, and I have not drank since. Nor do I ever want to drink again.

MT: Besides Lita, have you dated other women in the public eye?

CH: No.

MT: How many times have you had sex in your dressing room?

CH: I couldn't even tell you. With my wife? (laughs). I don't know. Really, I was hammered all of the time. Remember, I was married and when we were on the road, I didn't go out and fuck chicks because I wanted to be given the same respect that I gave her. And when someone asks me a question, if I lie, you can tell. I don't know why, it's always been that way.

MT: Tell us your worst groupie story.

CH: I was out in Atlantic City while I was dating Lita. I had lost $5,000 on two rolls of the dice. I held my head up high, went outside the casino, and bashed my face against the wall because that was all the money I had on me! (laughs). So, I went around the corner into this rock club. I was hammered. Some chick came up and started talking to me. She had mentioned W.A.S.P. to me. She asked if I wanted to get something to eat. We went and got some pizza. We went back to my room, and the phone rang. It was my old lady (Lita). She knew someone was there. I lied to her and told her there wasn't. Then when I hung up, I told the chick she had to split. It was just the weirdest fuckin' thing.

MT: What is the scariest STD you ever caught?

CH: It was syphilis. We were touring, and I noticed some sores on my arms. The sores won't show up where you have tattoos for some reason. Then it went away, but my nose was running and I thought I had a cold. My ears were plugged up. So in New York, the tour manager came up to me and said that the health department in San Francisco called him. He said that they had gotten my name from a girl who was dying of syphilis. I went down and had a blood test, and sure enough, it was positive. The doctor said if I wouldn't have caught it in the next two months, I would have been dead. And I didn't know I had it. It didn't hurt when I pissed. Nothing. Luckily, my name came up!

MT: What makes you laugh?

CH: My friends, and the jokes we play on people. Also, the kids in the audience. They're having such a good time. After a W.A.S.P. show we were signing autographs and this kid came up to me saying "Dude, dude, I have pictures of you on every wall in my bedroom." And I was busting up laughing. He says "Dude, you don't get it, you're all over my bedroom." And I was laughing, telling him, "I do get it, because at my mom's house growing up, I had pictures of my idols all over my bedroom! Johnny Winter, Hendrix, all of them." (laughs). It was funny to see how freaked out he was. (laughs).

MT: Do you feel that you have left your legacy on the Sunset Strip?

CH: I don't feel that I have, but a lot of people tell me that I have. Maybe because I was born here. This is my home. You know about a year ago, The Rainbow finally put a picture of me up on their bar wall after 30 years. (laughs)

MT: I heard that you were banned from The Rainbow? Why?

CH: Oh yeah. From 1991-1996. I guess they didn't really kick me out, they just wouldn't let me in! Which I guess is like being kicked out. I used to just go in there and cause trouble. I would walk up to a table that had ordered pizza, grab a slice and walk away. I wouldn't even say anything to them. The people who had ordered the pizza were like, "What the fuck was that?" I don't think they ever said anything because of my size.

MT: What city in the world has the hottest women, best food, best geographic scenery?

CH: Salt Lake City for women, Germany as a whole for food, Switzerland in general for scenery.

MT: When is the last time you paid for/changed your own guitar strings?

CH: Yesterday. I bought a box for $30 and changed them yesterday.

MT: Who do you listen to now? Who are you listening to in your car?

CH: I don't have a stereo in my car, but I listened to some Johnny Winter yesterday. I have jammed with him a lot over the years! (laughs).

MT: Who is the most overrated musician in rock'n'roll?

CH: Gene Simmons. He's a good entertainer and he's a ruthless businessman, but I think his musicianship is overrated.

MT: Have you ever gotten into a fist fight with a band mate?
CH: No. But, I have come close.

MT: What was the first item you bought from your first big payday?
CH: We got $5,000 when we signed our deal with W.A.S.P. Minutes after that, a bum on the street asked me for a dollar and I gave him $100 bill. But one time in Germany I was at a train station, and I was kind of hammered, and this guy asked me for some change. I gave this guy all of the change that I had in my pocket. He looked at the change and said, "This is too much." I said, "Don't worry about it. Keep it, Man!" Come to find out some of the coins were worth $20! (laughs). I gave the guy about $400. (laughs)

MT: Who is the one person that you run into knowing you're going to have a long night of partying ahead of you?
CH: Phil Campbell (Motorhead). Every time I run into Phil we just have a good time and chill for like two days with no obligations.

MT: If you had a crystal ball, what age would it tell us you live to?
CH: With my luck, I will see all of my friends pass before me and live to 90, like in The Green Mile. (laughs).

MT: Realizing this might be a guess, rank in order what you have spent the most amount of money on at life to date. Cigarettes, booze, drugs?
CH: Booze, drugs, cigarettes.

MT: Should marijuana be legalized?
CH: Sure. It should have been legalized a long time ago.

MT: How often do you smoke marijuana?
CH: As often as I can. (laughs). I don't have a pot license. I should though.

MT: Should W.A.S.P. be in the Rock and Roll Hall of Fame?
CH: Right now? No.

MT: If W.A.S.P. was inducted into the Rock and Roll Hall of Fame, would you go to the ceremony?
CH: Yeah. I'm at least half of the deal.

MT: When was the last time you were blown away by a band's live performance?
CH: I saw Ratt last year at the Key Club. They were amazing! Carlos was playing with them and they sounded awesome!

MT: Who is the toughest guy in rock'n'roll?
CH: The bass player for Metallica, Robert Trujillo. I wouldn't want to mess with him.

MT: The best rock album ever produced?
CH: *Sabbath Bloody Sabbath*, by Black Sabbath

MT: What advice would you provide to a kid who wants to play rock music for a living?
CH: DTA. Don't trust anybody. Also, don't let anyone mess with your self esteem.

MT: What are you working on now? How can people get a hold of you?
CH: Check me out at www.chrisholmesrocks.com. I will be going out on the road this year with Where Angels Suffer (W.A.S.). I believe we will be touring Europe. I have been working on an album with Phil "Philthy Animal" Taylor (Motorhead), where I have written some lyrics which I have enjoyed, and done some singing. It's called SCUM.

Oz with Stryper on their 25th Anniversary Tour at the House of Blues, Orlando Florida. October 2009. Photo by Craig O'Hagen.

Oz Fox

Lead Guitar

Past-Play Ground, Sin Dizzy

Present-Stryper, Bloodgood, Vinyl Tattoo

MT: When was your birth date?
OF: June 18, 1961.

MT: The city you were raised in?
OF: Whittier, California.

MT: The city you currently reside?
OF: Las Vegas, Nevada.

MT: Did you graduate high school?
OF: Yes, 1979.

MT: Marital status?
OF: Married.

MT: Any kids?
OF: Three.

MT: When did you pick up your first guitar?
OF: I was six years old.

MT: Do you remember the first time you realized that you wanted to play music for a living?
OF: Yes, I was under 10 years old. I used to play and sing for my family at gatherings. I would get money from my cousins and uncles when I sang or played. (laughs).

MT: Were you involved in Band or music classes in High School?
OF: I was in vocal jazz ensemble in high school.

MT: Is it true that the name "Oz" is actually in reference to Ozzy Osbourne?

OF: That is true. When I was in high school, I used to play backyard parties. We would play Black Sabbath songs, and I would try to imitate Ozzy's voice. So, all of my friends started calling me Oz.

MT: You received a phone call in 1983 from the Sweet brothers. Did you know them previously?

OF: Yes. We went to high school together. I actually met Robert in 7th grade at a lunch time gathering. Of course, later I hooked up with him. We jammed together in high school, and eventually they asked me to be in their band.

MT: What was the name of the band at the time? Was there a Christian theme at the time?

OF: It was called Roxx Regime. At that time there was no Christian theme.

MT: Prior to you joining the band, who played guitar for Roxx Regime?

OF: Scott Lane was the person that I replaced. C.C DeVille had also auditioned for Roxx Regime.

MT: During the early stages of the band, who came up with the idea to move forward as a Christian-themed band?

OF: Basically, we were all from Christian homes. We had a neighborhood friend that inspired us to dedicate our music and our talents to God. We re-dedicated our lives at that point, and decided that is what we would do. That was in 1983.

MT: In 1984, the band's name was changed to Stryper, and you released your first EP, *The Yellow and Black Attack*. Explain the significance the of yellow and black color theme with the band?

OF: There really was no significance in the very beginning. It was just that Robert had painted his drums yellow and black. It was actually painted in different shapes. As time went on, the heat began to morph the paint, and he changed the pattern to stripes. From there, Robert talked everyone into striping everything yellow and black.

MT: Who were the bands that you were sharing a bill with early on?

OF: We opened for a number of groups locally. Keel was one of them. We ended up becoming good friends with Ron as time went on. He had a lot to do with us getting into the scene because he let us open for him. We opened for Anthrax, and Raven. Zebra as well.

MT: Were their crowds supportive of Stryper's Christian theme?
OF: The Anthrax-Raven crowd definitely did not like us. They pretty much spit on us, and flipped us off the whole show. It wasn't a good scene. But, in some places we had quite a loyal following that would come to our shows. I'm not so sure that the fan base of the headlining acts accepted us as much, as we had our own set of fans there to support us.

MT: Whose idea was it to throw bibles into the audience?
OF: I think it was Robert's idea. It was either him or Michael Guido, who was kind of a chaplain guy who hung out with us.

MT: *Soldiers Under Command* was released in 1985, and became your first gold record. With the band's rapid rise in popularity, were you all leading a perfect Christian lifestyle at the time?
OF: I don't think that anyone has a perfect Christian lifestyle! (laughs). To be honest, we were very young in our faith. We were still kind of growing, so to speak. We did our best to stay away from things that were against what we believed in. I can't say that it was always perfect, but we certainly weren't drinking, or doing drugs, or sleeping around with girls.

MT: So there were no crazy backstage parties?
OF: No. I guess we were protected from all of that by the people that were surrounding us, so to speak. We had a good team of people that would kind of guard us from any of that, and not allow that element back stage. It wasn't too hard to stay away from it.

MT: Stryper's third album was released in 1986. *To Hell with the Devil* was nominated for a Grammy, and sold over two million copies. What were you doing to indulge a little at the time?
OF: The first thing I did was move from my one-bedroom apartment that was in a rundown area. I found a decent size house, nothing extravagant, and got myself into a mortgage. And then I bought a SUV truck, which was kind of nice to have. And of course recording equipment, audio equipment, whatever went along with what I did. But,

I wasn't really into jewelry or anything real extravagant. I still wore shorts and t-shirts. (laughs).

MT: Although Stryper's Christian theme was embraced by most, it wasn't by all. Tell of a display of disrespect that you experienced playing live?
OF: I want to say the worst situation that we have been in was a show in Holland that we did in Eindovan, with a bunch of metal bands. The whole crowd - I don't know how many thousands of people - booed us. They threw food at us. They had upside down crosses that they chanted with. (laughs). It was pretty rowdy. We got in and out pretty quick. We did our shortest songs, and that was it.

MT: How was the band getting along at this time? Did the Sweet brothers treat you and Tim Gaines as "equals"?
OF: I believe that they did. But, I do think that there were people that were trying to push them to be in control of everything. But the band started out as four members that had a chemistry. So, if there were any kind of situations like that, they were pretty much talked out, and worked out so that it wouldn't be that way.

Oz with Stryper at Diesel in Pittsburgh, March 2011.
Photo by SharonDominikPhotography.com.

MT: How did the writing process work in Stryper?

OF: For the most part, Michael was the song writing machine. That is his passion, song writing. There were times when it was mostly his writing, and maybe Robert would pen some lyrics. I would write songs and submit them. I would get maybe a song or two on an album. Rarely did we ever co-write, although there were two albums that we co-wrote on. One was the first album, *The Yellow and Black Attack*, the other one would be the album, *Against the Law*. Everything else was either Michael writing it, or myself coming up with a song. Really, the rule was supposed to be whoever came up with a song that would work for Stryper on the album we were doing at the time, would be used on the album.

MT: Do you feel that the publishing was split fairly?

OF: That was one of the things that was an issue. The reason that Michael would write on his own was because the Sweet family had their own family publishing deal, which didn't allow outside writers. So, I had to start my own publishing company called, Sir Oz Music. When I wrote songs, that's where the publishing would go to. Although later on, when we did *Against the Law* we had come up with Stryper Music, because we were writing together at that point.

MT: The album *In God We Trust* was released in 1988, and also went gold. However, some critics felt the album was over-produced and "glammy". Justifiable?

OF: Everybody has an opinion, and that opinion is subjective. I think that we did the best we could after the record label told us that they wanted a carbon copy of *To Hell with the Devil*, only with better production. So what do you do with that? (laughs).

MT: Stryper totally changed their sound, look, and message with your 1990 release, *Against the Law*. Who spearheaded the drastic change?

OF: I would have to say a lot of that had to do with the record label. At the time, Guns N' Roses, Nirvana and these other raw sounding bands were getting very popular. This was during the grunge movement. So, our label highly suggested that we go back to our roots and do something more heavy sounding and raw, and that is why that album sounded the way it did. We also changed our look. We wanted to do something different than the spandex look or image. We were trying to graduate to something different, which I don't think that our fans accepted it very well, and it ended up biting us.

MT: Stryper released a Greatest Hits album in 1991, and then while Stryper was touring in support of it, Michael Sweet left the band to start a solo career. Did you see this coming?
OF: At that point, no. I did not see it coming. We were brought into a meeting which, at the time, was the Stryper office that we don't have any longer. Michael sat down with Janice Sweet, who was our manager at the time, and said, "I'm quitting." He wanted to go on and do a solo project. For whatever reason, he didn't have faith in the band at that time, and didn't want to continue.

MT: How did you like continuing the tour as a three-piece band playing guitar and singing most nights?
OF: Well, I am no Michael Sweet. I can't sing like him, especially on all of our songs. I plucked out the ones that I knew I could sing, and we pulled off a set. That is basically what it was all about. I did do it, and the people accepted it, and we did it again. The first time was in Europe, and then we were asked to come back to Europe as a three-piece, so we did. We were thinking about what we would do for a new singer. I think we auditioned a handful of guys to sing, but ultimately I thought it would be best if I took over the vocals. Robert didn't want to do that, so I left the band.

MT: Robert carried on using the Stryper name for a while, but it had lost its traction. You started Sin Dizzy with Tim Gaines? Will we ever hear more from Sin Dizzy?
OF: No, Sin Dizzy is pretty much a done deal and has been done for a while. I have no plans to continue doing any Sin Dizzy projects.

MT: Years later in 2003, Stryper reunited. Since then, the band has been on numerous tours and produced three studio albums. Do you have a favorite?
OF: *The Covering* is probably my favorite of the three. It was a real interesting way to show people where our roots came from. And I was able to cut loose a little bit on it myself, and do some things that were a little bit different and more my real style of playing. Whereas, with most Stryper songs; I am mostly directed on what I should play.

MT: You have been playing in a couple side projects as well. Vinyl Tattoo and Bloodgood. What are your current music priorities in order?
OF: Right now, obviously Stryper is a big priority to me. Probably first and foremost. When I am not doing Stryper, I am working hard on

a guitar instructional video website, called Sir Oz Academy. Those two things are probably my biggest priorities. When I am not playing or touring with Stryper, if all of the members of Vinyl Tattoo are in town, we play gigs in Las Vegas or the Southwestern area of the country. Bloodgood is extremely seasonal. We don't do that many dates, but when we do it's quite an event and I love being a part of it. We're actually working on some tracks to re-release one of the albums called, *All Stand Together*. I am adding my guitar tracks to the album and it will be re-released.

MT: You appear to be very supportive and involved in your wife's non-profit organization. Can you tell us about it?
OF: Yes, I am very involved with my wife in all of her activities with her organization called, Hookers for Jesus. Which is an organization that helps women get out of prostitution, which actually is sex trafficking. If you study how prostitution happens, you realize that these girls get trapped. Even though they may choose that profession, they get trapped and become slaves to pimps and live a life of tyranny. Some of them are even killed or die due to drug overdoses. I try to participate whenever I am home, or I can schedule it, to do whatever I can to help them. First and foremost, we help them get out of that business. That's the priority. Get them out of that, and help them escape the life. Once they have escaped, they are so used to making $500 in 10 minutes, and are not used to working a normal job. At that point, we do everything we can to encourage them. Help them get to church, help them with their bills, and hopefully get them on the road to a normal life, so that they don't have to return to prostitution.

Oz and wife, Annie Lobert. April 2012.

MT: Presently, how important is your faith to you?
OF: At this point, my faith is the most important thing in my life. My belief in God who we believe sent Jesus Christ as his son for sacrifice for all sins…I put him on the throne of my life. Everything that is in my life, including me, gets put in order that way. In proper order.

MT: Do you like living in Las Vegas?
OF: It's the entertainment capital of the world for me. I love it!

MT: If you were asked to do MTV's Cribs, would you do it?
OF: I don't have a crib for them to do! (laughs).

MT: How big is your current place you call home?
OF: I couldn't even tell you the square footage. I live in a two-bedroom apartment, let's just say that.

MT: What kind of car(s) do you own?
OF: I have a 1996 Cobra Mustang that was a gift. It was from a very good friend, Ray Schneiders. He is a retired police officer from the Fontana Police Department. I produced his son's band, and that is one reason he gave me the car on my birthday as a gift. He was retiring and he was getting himself a new vehicle, so he decided he wanted to give me the car.

MT: Are you in a financial situation that you never have to work again?
OF: Absolutely not.

MT: Are you registered to vote? Will you be voting in November (2012)? Who for?
OF: Yes, Yes, not Obama! I am a Republican.

MT: Do you have a guilty pleasure?
OF: I think my only guilty pleasure is overeating.

MT: What band mate from Stryper do you hang out with the most?
OF: (laughs). Probably Michael.

MT: Do you smoke cigarettes?
OF: No.

MT: Did you have a drug of choice back in the day?
OF: No. I really never did drugs. I tried smoking pot when I was 15, and I ended up being allergic to it. I never tried it again.

MT: When you're on tour, how much do you get for your food per diem each day?
OF: It varies between $25-$35 a day.

MT: Do you have a pre-gig warm up ritual?
OF: I mostly warm up on 3 note per string mode scale patterns before shows.

MT: What beverage do you drink during a show?
OF: Water.

MT: What do you think of making videos?
OF: I think that videos are important, but you can spend a lot of time making videos, and they are *grueling*. A video can take up to 20 hours to film. I didn't look forward to them.

MT: What is the most eccentric thing on your rider with Stryper?
OF: I think that most people would be surprised to know that all we ever ask for is some granola bars, water, and fruit! (laughs).

MT: Have you ever been concerned for your safety while on stage performing?
OF: You are kind of vulnerable any time you are on stage, but the only thing that really concerns me is when you get shocked because you are plugged into your amp with a cord and touching the microphone with the ground loop. That's no fun. Sometimes when that happens you see blue lights in your eyes. That's how bad it can get.

MT: Does that happen only in wet conditions?
OF: No, no. It can happen in dry conditions, especially when your equipment is not on the same ground system as the audio system. What ends up happening is your body becomes the conduit between two grounds. So, if you go up and put your lips on a microphone when you aren't using a wireless system, you can get heavy shock to your body.

MT: Should marijuana be legalized?
OF: I don't think so.

MT: Should Stryper be in The Rock and Roll Hall of Fame?
OF: My honest opinion is yes. We do belong in The Rock and Roll Hall of Fame.

MT: What advice would you provide to a guitar player who wants to play rock music for a living?
OF: Be ready to struggle financially! (laughs). Play all of the time, and go to Sir Oz Academy and learn your modes.

MT: What are you working on now?
OF: I am working on Sir Oz Academy, www.sirozacademy.com. It is a subscription online video library. You can access all kinds of instruction videos there that are all about the way I play, and the reason why I play the way I play. I will also be adding gear and equipment information. There will be interviews from other artists on there, and I will continue to progress with more videos as time goes on. Every month I add videos. We have introductory pricing right now on the site, which is $24.99 per month for the first two months, minimum. But then it's just $10.99 per month after that.

Lips at Erie Canal Harbor in Buffalo, New York. August 2011.
*Photo by © Dalila Kriheli * rockstarpix.com*

Steve "Lips" Kudlow

Lead Vocals/Lead Guitar

Present-Anvil

MT: When was your birth date?
SK: March 2, 1956.

MT: The city you were raised in?
SK: Toronto.

MT: The city you currently reside?
SK: Toronto.

MT: Did you graduate high school?
SK: Yes, in 1974.

MT: Marital status?
SK: Married.

MT: Any kids?
SK: I have two step children, and one son.

MT: When was the first time you picked up a guitar?
SK: It was during the summer when I was 10 years old.

MT: Were you involved in music classes in high school?
SK: Yes. In grade seven, I got stuck into Vocal class because I screwed up a music test going into junior high. (laughs). It was sort of a logistical mistake. It was one of those old computer tests that you filled your answers in with a black lead pencil. The way the columns were set up was confusing. I ended up answering the right questions in the wrong column! So they put me into Vocal class, which I don't resent. Eventually I talked the guidance counselor into putting me into Strings class for the next year. So, in grade eight, I played violin.

MT: How did you get the nickname, Lips?

SK: That came from Robb's (Reiner, Drums) dad. I was always talking a lot, and had something to say about everything, and he just started calling me that.

MT: You and Robb Reiner first jammed back in 1973, and years later in 1978, you had put together a solid four-piece band. Is it true that an early version of Anvil was called Lips?

SK: Absolutely. That was what we originally called the band until we put out our first album. The reason that we changed the name was that the record company didn't want any confusion with the band Lips Incorporated or Horse Lips.

MT: In 1981, the band changed its name to Anvil, released their first album, *Hard 'N' Heavy,* and signed with Attic Records. What was the vision for Anvil at that time?

SK: I don't think that it was any different than it is today - to make music that we love. It was a simple as that. Robb and I grew up on very, very hard music. That is what we planned on doing for a lifetime, and not giving in on it.

MT: After the album came out, is it true that you received a phone call from Lemmy?

SK: That was actually after our second album, *Metal on Metal*. It wasn't actually Lemmy who called, it was his management. They had some problems with "Fast" Eddie Clarke and they wanted me to come in, finish the tour, and possibly do the next album. But I couldn't do it, because of course, I was already in Anvil.

MT: Although commercial success was hard to come by in your home country of Canada, Anvil had a huge following in other areas, especially Europe. Why do you think metal fans are so passionate in Europe?

SK: I don't think that there is really an explanation for it. I think that it is very simply, environment. That environment is much more of a music culture to begin with. In actual fact, if you really stop and think about it, that is where all of music originates from anyways. You really can't analyze it and figure it out. It's just the way it is.

Lips and toy during the Canadian Coast to Coast Tour,
*May 2011. Photo by Dalila Kriheli * rockstarpix.com*

MT: Anvil was known for their high energy stage show, and fast heavy metal riffs. When did you begin experimenting playing your guitar with a sex toy?
SK: (laughs). Immediately! When Robb and I had decided that we would put this all original band together, we decided that the songs were all going to be about sex. Being in your late teens and early twenties, that's all you think about anyway. (laughs). I came into rehearsal with the idea that I would play my guitar with a vibrator because the sound of the motor would come through my pick-ups. I also thought that it could be used as a bottle neck, because it was a hard plastic surface that was round. That is how that came to be.

MT: After a gig at The Marquee Club in London in 1982, you met a rabid Anvil fan, 15 year-old Sacha Gervasi. What do you remember about meeting Sacha for the first time?
SK: We had gone to London with the promise that we were going to play The Monsters of Rock Donington Festival, two nights at The Marquee, and a supposed tour with Def Leppard. This is what the record company told us. This was the first time we had ever been

overseas so it was extraordinarily exciting. We played Donington first, and then we had the two nights at The Marquee in London. After the first night at The Marquee, there was a knock at the changing room door, and this kid walks in. Meanwhile, the room is packed with guys from the music industry. Guys from Twisted Sister, Fastway and others are hanging out drinking our beer and eating our food! (laughs). What's funny is that Robb and I end up in a conversation with this kid. And the kid seems to know more about us than anyone in the room! (laughs). We found ourselves wanting to talk with this kid more than the musicians there to drink our beer. He made us promise that he would be able to take us to Carnaby Street the next day to show us where to buy the bullet belts and paraphernalia that you would get for heavy metal at the time. We went out with him the next day and found out that he had relatives living in Toronto. It was a weird kind of synchronicity. During the summers he would fly to Toronto to see his aunts and uncles, or to New York to visit his dad. So he started telling us that he was going to come visit us in Toronto. So we gave him our address and the next thing you know, Sacha is in Toronto banging on my door! (laughs). This kid was becoming a really good friend, and since he played drums and was such an avid fan, we decided to ask him to come out on the road with us doing tours around Quebec. So he came on the road with us, and remember, in those days, it was party central. It was insane! I remember he met this beautiful little French girl and takes her into the back of the van, and he has his first experience of life like that, you know? (laughs)

MT: In 1983, Anvil signed with Aerosmith's manager, David Krebs, after convincing Attic to release you from your contract. Did Krebs give Anvil the attention that he promised during the signing process?
SK: It was David Krebs that got us out of our contract with Attic, and no. He was too busy and I think that he kind of lost interest. And to be quite honest, I don't think that he really understood exactly what we were. He was still a little old school. He really didn't give us the attention, and the attention that he did give us and the direction he somewhat pointed in was very, very detrimental to what needed to happen. At the end of the day it was the wrong guy at the wrong time. But if you look at things in the sense that everything happens for a reason, then you would have said to him what I said to David when I saw him again 25 years later, which was "Thank you for screwing up my career because I wouldn't be here now had you not!" (laughs)

MT: An entirely different Rob Reiner directed "This is Spinal Tap" in 1984. What did you think of the movie the first time you saw it?

SK: I loved it. But, I thought it was a total rip of the movie "Bad News Tour". I think it was made for TV originally. It was an English movie and quite similar. Understand that they are vastly different levels of movies. "Bad News Tour" is a lot more raw. "Spinal Tap" is a much more polished version.

MT: During this time, heavy metal was incredibly popular world-wide. Was there a particular band or two that passed Anvil up that you just didn't understand?

SK: No, not really. I suppose in a certain sense, I was a bit surprised at the end of the day with Metallica. I had met them before their first album came out. I listened to their first album, and I think I was a bit surprised that it got as big as it did, but I didn't begrudge it. Bands like Iron Maiden and Judas Priest had such pristine, beautiful, incredible vocals. When I listened to Metallica it wasn't like that. At that point, I would have never thought that Metallica would be bigger than Judas Priest. I'm not saying that James is a bad vocalist - I am not saying that at all. What I mean is very simply, Rob Halford, Ronnie Dio, Bruce Dickenson - these are great metal vocalists. They are the bar. But on the other side of that, I think Metallica's popularity is great because it means that it is not necessarily the ability, it's the character, and that's fine too.

MT: Krebs released Anvil from their contract in 1986, unable to sign the band to a major label. In 1987, Anvil signed with Metal Blade. Anvil released three albums on the label, including *Strength of Steel* which was the bands most commercially successful album in the US. How did you end up on Metal Blade?

SK: William Howell, who is now known as DJ Will with KNAC, was working with Metal Blade at the time, and had gotten a hold of the *Strength of Steel* demo tapes. He started calling me once a week wanting to sign us. I put that guy through the ringer for six months, man. And that's no shit. I didn't want to go with Metal Blade, man. That was like our last choice. I just thought it was no better, if not worse, than what we had already experienced, and I really didn't want to go there. But, at the end of the day, we were getting refusals from everyone. Some places you would send the tape, and they would send it back with a note saying, "Sorry, we don't accept unsolicited material." They wouldn't even accept the tape! And that's after I made a phone call to someone saying, "I am sending you a tape." Unsolicited? Didn't I call you? You said, "Send me the tape!" (laughs). Some of the stuff that I dealt with was incredible. I remember at the time, I sent CBS the demo tape and they said, "We already have Judas Priest. You sound too much like them." One of the labels wanted us to change our name, saying that we were too old. So, the next time William called me, I said, "Ok, let's have a look at the contract. Send it over." We ended up doing three releases through Metal Blade.

MT: Was music a full time job at that point?
SK:　Yes, it was. But at the cost of my first marriage. (laughs)

MT: After Metal Blade, you signed with Maximum Records, then Massacre Records releasing five albums between 1992-2001. Anvil continued to tour in support of the albums to sparse crowds at times. You were quoted in 2001 as saying, "We'll play gigs sometimes where there is no one is there." Did you ever feel like calling it quits?
SK:　No. It's just like owning a hardware store. You can do no business on some days. Does that mean you should close the store? That was exactly our situation. You know what? Even after the movie and everything Anvil has done, there have still been situations where we are still playing to 10 people. Why? Because it's a fuckin' Monday night, and no one knew we were there. It's not that the band isn't popular, it's because sometimes nothing has been done to let people know that we are there.

MT: In 2002, Anvil went back to Attic Records and released the bands 11th album, *Still Going Strong*, which received mostly positive reviews. However, the lyrics were viewed by many reviewers as poorly written. What are your thoughts when you hear such criticism?
SK:　I don't really recall that. Oh, now that you are mentioning it we had a song called "Waiting" on *Still Going Strong*. A critic said, "What a useless terrible subject!" Some people, if they don't relate to what you are saying, man, they go nuts.

MT: *Back to Basics* was released in 2004, and it too received positive reviews. But Anvil cancelled their previously announced tour of Eastern Canada in support of the album. What was the cancellation based on?

168

SK: No money. There was a guy from an agency in Toronto that tried to book some shows for us out east. When we looked at it, it was impossible to do. You have to be able to afford to go on tour. It was going to cost us a fortune. It's not that we weren't going to make enough, it was just going to cost us too much. (laughs). I'm the type of person that I will do anything if it doesn't cost me. If it breaks even, I'm on my way!

MT: Late 2004 was arguably the lowest point for the band. You were working for a catering company, and Anvil still had very little acknowledgement in Canada. Out of the blue you received an email from your old roadie, Sacha Gervasi. What was the reason for his email?

SK: We still don't know. It was as simple as he was listening to a Metallica album and thought of us. He emailed me, and that is how it all got started. I had no idea what he had been up to, so it was quite shocking. I emailed him my phone number, and he called me back within a couple minutes. We spoke for a while, and he wanted me to fly to LA to visit with him. It wasn't around the corner, so I didn't think I was going to be making the trip. He said, "No, no. I am going to pay for it. Don't worry about it." The next day, the FedEx truck pulled up with tickets to LA! I went down the following weekend. He picked me up at the airport in his Jaguar. Here is the kid that I knew, but as a grown man. His eyes had the same sparkle, and it's hard to explain, but it was like not even a day had passed. He began to tell me that he worked as a screenwriter for Steven Spielberg. This was my little buddy, and it was great to see him again. We ended up cruising around and rekindling our friendship. It was really like no time had passed at all. The friendship that we all had was very organic and special. That weekend he took me to another screenwriter's house, his friend, Steve Zaillian. Steve was involved recently with "American Gangster", "Moneyball", and others. He is a very successful screenwriter. Sacha and Steve are dear friends, and he took me over there. It was Steve, I think, who sparked the idea to Sacha to take a look at what he had in front of him, and maybe make a movie about it. For whatever reason, Sacha felt compelled to help us. He said, "There must be something I can do to help make your career what it should be." He felt that it was an incredible injustice. I'm going, "What do you mean an incredible injustice? I'm doing fine." He was like, "You don't get it. You should be ten times bigger than Metallica!"

MT: A week later he flew to Toronto and called a meeting with you. Did you have any idea what news he was bringing to this meeting?

SK: No. He asked me to pick him up at the airport like I did 25 years earlier and take him to his uncle's place. (laughs). So there we are in his uncle's living room, and he drops this on me. He was going to make a movie about Anvil. I completely lost it. There were all kinds of premonitions that happened before that actual moment, and I knew that the winds of change were upon me. It's hard to explain, but it happened at a festival a week before Sacha contacted me. This was the festival that Ivan met Tiziana. That was where we made the contact for the tour that got into the movie…two of the guys that I met on that initial walk around London with Sacha 25 years earlier had joined a band called Candlemass that was headlining this festival that we were playing at in Italy.

MT: Did you guys talk money during this meeting? Was there an advance payment, or were you to receive a percentage of the gross?

SK: There was never any conversation about money. This had nothing to do with money. This was a pure act of generosity on the behalf of everybody involved. *Everybody* involved. Everybody did it for the sake of doing it with hopes that it would work. If there was money, we would share it. That's how it was done. All on Sacha's good nature and his pocketbook.

MT: Sacha started shooting "Anvil! The Story of Anvil" in 2005. The criticism of most reality TV is that it is totally scripted, and not "reality" at all. Were any of the "Spinal Tap-esque" events that Anvil encountered in the documentary scripted?

SK: No. There were no scripted parts. If it comes across as scripted it was a matter of editing. Editing took over a year as there was over 320 hours of footage. (laughs). It *needed* to be edited.

MT: Were there any experiences that you encountered during the filming that you asked Sacha to not include in the final film?

SK: The only thing that I complained about was the nude picture of myself standing in the doorway. It was a picture that Ross Halfin took of me in 1983 standing in the doorway of a motel. I didn't want that in the movie.

MT: In 2007, Anvil released their 13th studio album, *This is Thirteen*. The documentary was released in 2008 at the Sundance Film Festival to high praise and acclaim. I've got to ask. Were you able to pay your sister, Rhonda, back for the loan she gave you to produce *This is Thirteen*?

SK: Absolutely. It didn't take long after Sundance to do that. Rhonda came to Sundance and we began paying her back right there! After the first night that the movie showed, out in the freezing cold and snow blizzard, we opened up the back of a van in the parking lot that was filled with *This is Thirteen* CDs, and blasted the music from it. Everyone gathered around the van, and bought CDs at $20 each. We had old people coming up saying, "I have never bought a heavy metal CD in my life, but I want to buy two to support you." It really didn't take very long.

MT: The success of the documentary has put Anvil back on the map, making the band more popular than ever 30 plus years after the bands formation. How has the documentary changed your life?

SK: In a certain sense, all that it has done is it removed what I hated to do, which was the deliveries for the catering company. That is basically all it changed, where I am making money from. It might not be a big thing to some people, but it's a huge thing to me because now I don't have to do that in order to survive. The word is *survive*. It's not about making millions of dollars. It never has been, and more than likely, it never will be. Hopefully, I'm working at it. On the reality side, I am making a living just like everyone else.

MT: Who were some of the first music gear companies who wanted your endorsement after the success of the movie?

SK: Gibson. Right from the onset of Sundance. They were one of the first companies to step up. They have been extraordinarily nice to me. Not in the sense that they have given me a lot of guitars...some of them I buy, some I have been lucky enough that they have given them to me. But in the bigger scheme of things, they have helped promote the movie. Recently we were nominated for a JUNO Award and Gibson stepped up and chauffeured us around to the JUNO Awards in the Gibson Tour Bus. How awesome is that? I'm not pulling up to the JUNO Awards in a limo, I'm coming in a tour bus! (laughs)

MT: How much has your concert merchandise sales changed in the last four years?
SK: That's where I am making my living from. The bigger you get, the more you need, and the bigger your expenses get. So, now when we go on the road, we might get paid more but it's costing us more to tour. Your road crew gets bigger; you have to rent more or larger vehicles, more equipment, et cetera. You have to add all this stuff to the tour which costs more money, which is why you are getting paid more for your gigs. So how are we making our money? Find out how many t-shirts we sold tonight?! (laughs). I laugh about it because I say that I am in the same business as my dad, who was a tailor. I sell garments!

MT: The last few years you have toured as a three-piece band, eliminating the rhythm guitar spot. Do you foresee ever bringing back a second guitar player?
SK: No. In reality, it was never part of the fundamental aspect of the band. It became more of a dead weight, and it was something that wasn't necessary.

MT: In a perfect world, would you prefer just being the lead guitarist or lead vocalist of Anvil rather than both?
SK: That is an interesting question. No, I think I need to be both. I think that is kind of what I am destined to do. I think initially I didn't want to sing. But after getting punched in the kidneys by a singer, I decided that I am never going to work with a singer again and I am going to have to learn to do it myself. I am never going to have to depend on an idiot like that again.

MT: Is there a music act that you would jump at the chance to sing or play guitar in if it meant giving up Anvil?
SK: No. That would be giving up myself, and I won't do that.

MT: If you or Robb chose to leave Anvil, could the band continue as Anvil?
SK: No.

MT: In 2011, Anvil released the album, *Juggernaut of Justice*, which was recorded at Dave Grohl's studio in Northridge, CA. Why did you choose to use Dave's studio?
SK: He chose us! (laughs). As a result of the movie, we ended up being nominated for an Independent Spirit Award and were to play at Independent Spirit Awards as well. VH1 had called Dave up to see if

he wanted to introduce Anvil at the awards show, and he went nuts! "Boy would I ever!" This was unbeknownst to us, and the only indication that we had that Dave Grohl might be interested in Anvil was the fact that he did the album *Probot*, which we thought in our own little world, "It sounds like he has been listening to us." And then we kind of laughed. We didn't take it too serious. So, the night of the awards, Dave pulls up in his limo. He gets out and he was carrying this guitar case. The first thing that comes to my mind is, "Amazing! Dave is going to come up and play "Metal on Metal" with us!" He comes up and puts the guitar case down beside me and says, "This is a Dave Grohl Gibson semi-hollow. You are probably the only other guitar player in the world that uses a semi-hollow guitar. You're going to appreciate this. I love you, Lips. I always have." And he hugs me. He says, "This is for you." He has given me one of his guitars! I was like, "What? What? What?!" I was just freaking out. Of course, later he went up and did our introduction. He talked about being at the right place at the right time, and that he got lucky with Nirvana. He went on to say that, "This is another point in my life that I am at the right spot at the right time because I get to introduce Anvil to America." In a certain sense, you know? It was really a heartfelt speech that he gave, and of course we played, and it was incredible. Everyone from Elton John to Christopher Plummer was in the audience, and here we are playing, "Metal on Metal"! Afterwards we were standing backstage and Dave came up to us and says, "You have to come to my studio and record. It's pro bono, boys. And if you don't take me up on this offer, I will never talk to you again!" (laughs). Needless to say, he pushed aside projects that were going on to open up the studio for us to use when it was convenient for us. It felt very, very nice to be there with the big, huge Motorhead flag in the recording room. It had the essence of being the real deal.

MT: Let's jump to some personal questions. How do you feel the last night of a long tour?
SK: I am always really sad to see it end. It always ends way too early. I always feel that way.

MT: Do you watch the other bands that you share on a bill with before or after your gig?
SK: Yeah. I watch them before and after.

MT: Do you live in the same house that you lived in featured in the documentary?
SK: Yes.

MT: What size is it?
SK: Four bedrooms, two-story.

MT: What kind of car do you drive?
SK: I drive my late father's car. I inherited it. It's the car that I am driving at the beginning of the movie. It's a Chrysler Concorde, 1998. It's like brand new. My dad only drove it in the summer time. When I got the car in 2005, it had 50,000 kilometers on it, which is like 30,000 miles.

MT: Are you in a financial position that you never have to work again?
SK: No.

MT: Do you smoke cigarettes?
SK: I guess you could say I do. It's usually mixed with pot. When I smoke tobacco, I mix it with pot. I don't really differentiate the two. They are both treated like a drug to me. It's like alcohol. I administer if and when I want to. It's nothing really habitual.

MT: Do you ever smoke just a tobacco cigarette?
SK: Seldom. It's usually when I run out of pot!

MT: How often are you recognized in public?
SK: Very often. People will typically want a picture or an autograph.

MT: What was your drug of choice back in the day?
SK: Pot. It still is.

MT: If you took a drug test today, what would it tell us?
SK: That I still smoke pot! (laughs)

MT: Should marijuana be legalized?
SK: Absolutely.

MT: Do you follow sports?
SK: Not really.

MT: How is your health?
SK: Very good.

MT: Is there a band that you have toured with who you did not get along with?
SK: Iced Earth. I'm not going to feed the fire, except to say that he wasn't nice to us. He wasn't nice to anybody.

MT: Who do you listen to in your car?
SK: I listen to oldies. Big band, swing. I love the 50's, 60's, and 70's. And I listen to Anvil. I listen to the *Juggernaut* album. I have it in the cassette player because it's a car from the 90's. I have it on both sides of the cassette so that I never have to flip it over.

MT: Do you have a pre-gig, warm up ritual?
SK: Water. I drink a lot of water.

MT: What beverage do you drink during a show?
SK: Water. Room temperature water. Only very seldom do I drink alcohol.

MT: What is the most eccentric thing on your rider?
SK: Socks. Black socks. We wear them, and then we throw them out. This way you don't have to wash socks. They are only like a buck a pair, or whatever. You tell them to bring you four pairs at every gig, and you change your socks. You throw out your old ones from the night before.

MT: Who is the one person that you run into knowing you're going to have a long night of partying ahead of you?
SK: I had a really good time drinking - and I don't drink very often - with Lemmy. If I was going to sit down with Lemmy, it would be a long night of drinking.

MT: Do you know Lemmy very well?
SK: He's like family in a certain sense, but estranged. But family, none the less. And those are his words. We're very respectful and loving of each other, I suppose.

MT: Should Anvil be in The Rock and Roll Hall of Fame?
SK: I don't know. That is not for me to decide.

MT: While on tour, have you ever called a city by the wrong name?
SK: Yes! (laughs). I realized it right after I did it. I didn't even try to cover for it. I just made fun of myself.

MT: If it were a simple process, would you remove any of your tattoos?
SK: I have only got two, and I would keep them both.

MT: When was the last time you were blown away by a band's live performance?
SK: I am almost embarrassed to say. Green Day. I think they are one of the best live bands I have seen, ever.

Lips in Ontario, Canada December 2011.
Photo by © Dalila Kriheli *Rock Star Pix.com

MT: The best rock album ever made?
SK: Probably, *Are you Experienced* by Jimi Hendrix.

MT: What advice would you provide to a player who wants to play rock music for a living?
SK: I would learn how to not necessarily be the best, but be the most unique and individual musician that you could possibly be. Come up with new ideas, and be innovative. Otherwise, it's just redundant. It won't mean a thing. You have to write songs and create music that no one can do but you. That's what the job really is. It's not about being the best, it's about being unique.

MT: What are you working on now?

SK: Please take a look at our latest CD, *Juggernaut of Justice*. I think that it is the greatest thing that we have ever done. I want people to know about it. I don't think I can talk about it enough. Also, Anvil's Metal Pounders Union. It's our extended family that also includes every other metal band. It's like a fan club, but it's different than a regular fan club because each person is given a specific ID number, and they must validate by photograph. So, everybody is identifiable to everybody else. Everybody gets to know each other. It's like a family. Recently, Scott Ian and David Ellefson joined. Alice Cooper, the Twisted Sister guys, and Tony Iommi have been members for a while. It is continually growing, and it's not just famous people, it's everybody. People are connecting through this from all over the world. We do lotteries for each city that we go to where people can win free tickets to our shows. Also, if you have a card at one of our gigs, it's an automatic Meet N Greet. You get to meet us, period.

Betsy promo photo for Bitch, September 2010.
Photo by John Morgan

Betsy Bitch

Lead Vocals

Past-The Boxboys

Present-Bitch, Betsy Bitch & The Knockers

MT: What is your birthdate?
BB: August 1, 1957.

MT: The city you were raised in?
BB: Brigantine, New Jersey. Right across the bridge from Atlantic City.

MT: The city you currently reside?
BB: Studio City, California.

MT: Marital Status?
BB: Single.

MT: Any children?
BB: No. Two dogs. A male and a female.

MT: How old were you the first time you were told that you had a great voice?
BB: It would have been my senior year in high school. I was singing back up in a band that played at parties and churches. I was about 16 and that was when I first got a sense of my good pitch and impressive projection.

MT: Were you involved in "Choir" type classes in high school?
BB: Yes, I was involved in Glee Club back then.

MT: Who were your influences at that time?
BB: In terms of performance, Alice Cooper. In terms of vocal inspiration, Robin Zander of Cheap Trick.

MT: Did you graduate high school?
BB: Almost. I think I was 15 credits short of graduating.

MT: What did you aspire to do after high school?
BB: I always aspired to front a rock band. I wanted to be a lead singer. Music, particularly rock music, is something that I have had passion for since my early teens.

MT: In 1980, you answered an ad in the Music Connection for a singer placed by Bitch founders, David Carruth and Robby Settles. Is it true that they had their heart set on a male vocalist early on?
BB: I wouldn't say they had their heart set on it. They just had the mindset that they would be an all male band called, Bitch. They really hadn't considered a female vocalist until I answered the ad, and eventually got the gig. They really weren't at all opposed to the idea, and then they realized, what better name for a female-fronted metal band.

MT: Bitch was formed in late 1980, and your first gig was six months later opening for Dante Fox (later became Great White) at the Troubadour. What do you remember about that night?
BB: I actually remember a lot about that night. Although we went on after Dante Fox, they were billed as the headliner, and since we took the stage at midnight on a Sunday night, in reality, they did have the better time slot. I remember that we had to share a dressing room with them and they wouldn't vacate to give me my privacy while I changed into my stage clothes. I ended up having to change while my sister held a towel up in front of me as best she could. We played a great show, and even though the hour was late, a good part of the crowd stuck around to see us. I recall that night knowing in my heart that we had the start of something really cool.

MT: Shortly after your first gig, your guitar player (David Carruth) met Brian Slagel who was putting together a compilation album of unknown metal artists. What were your thoughts when you learned Bitch would have a song on that album?
BB: I met Brian through David. Brian was working at Oz Records, a small "mom and pop" record store that specialized in the best selection of metal imports, picture discs, rare and obscure releases, etc., which David was an avid collector of. We were excited about being on the *Metal Massacre* release because we knew it would give us more

national and international exposure than merely being a local band playing the Los Angeles club circuit that would facilitate.

MT: *Metal Massacre* #1 (*MM*) was released in 1982. What did *MM*'s release do to Bitch's popularity?
BB: It gave us some much needed exposure and publicity, and got us noticed. It was definitely very advantageous for the band.

MT: Who was Bitch sharing a bill with at the time?
BB: Most of the bands that we were on Metal Blade with, such as Armored Saint, Slayer, Metallica, Ratt, Malice, etc. Metallica actually opened for us in San Francisco. This was when Dave Mustaine was in the band. He was a real upstart back then. I remember the club we played, The Stone in San Francisco, provided each band with a case of beer in their dressing room, and our case ended up missing. Although we didn't know for sure, our suspicions led us to believe that Dave swiped it. Outside of that, we got along great with all of the bands that we shared a bill with. We were all one big happy Metal Blade family.

MT: Was there any envy on the Sunset Strip from bands not included on *MM*?
BB: If there was, it was never really brought to our attention. Although, during a gig one night, this all-girl metal band decided to harass me for no apparent reason, other than the fact that they may have seen me as competition and felt threatened. They all stood there glaring at me. Then they started throwing ice cubes at me! It was crazy. They eventually apologized and we actually became friends after that, but that was a wild night. Hey, I'm a lover not a fighter.

MT: Shortly after the release of *MM*#1, Bitch released the EP, *Damnation Alley*, in 1982 and followed that with a full length album, *Be My Slave*, in 1983. What are your thoughts on those two albums?
BB: I am proud of both albums. Outside of a single that I cut with another band, *Damnation Alley* was my first real experience in the studio. I really like the songs on that EP. *Be My Slave* was very cool as well, but we had booked studio time in advance and I had a bad cold the entire time we were recording. I somehow got through it, but my voice wasn't 100% and I know I could have sung better, however, there wasn't much we could do in terms of re-scheduling as the studio time was already booked by Brian and Metal Blade, so I made the best of it. The sound on the album was a bit thin, but recently Metal Blade has

re-mixed, re-mastered and re-released *Be My Slave* and it sounds awesome!

MT: Do you still listen to those two albums?
BB: I do listen to them on occasion. Probably a little bit more now since *Be My Slave* has been re-mastered.

MT: While supporting *Be My Slave*, Bitch developed their controversial stage show that included S&M themes, including the humiliation of a male slave on stage. Whose idea was the stage show?
BB: Shortly after we got together and the songs had begun to get written, the image just sort of evolved in keeping with the subject matter of the songs. The same is true for the stage show. After we experimented with the image and props, we decided to take it one level up with the theatrics. It gave us an edge because it gave the audience an entertaining visual to go along with the kick-ass music they were hearing.

MT: How much was Bitch gigging at the time? Were all gigs in/around LA?
BB: We were playing on a fairly regular basis - probably about six times a month. Mostly we played in LA, although we played in San Diego as well as San Francisco on occasion. We also played a two-gig weekend in Queens, New York.

MT: About this time, the heavy metal movement on the Sunset Strip was exploding. How often were you on the Strip hanging out? What was it like?
BB: It was incredible. I was in Hollywood practically seven nights a week. You wouldn't even necessarily have to go into the clubs, because there was a party on the street. All of the bands would be walking around handing out flyers for their next gig, socializing and networking. Every night there were great bands playing somewhere on the Sunset Strip and other clubs in Hollywood. I have fond memories of that time.

MT: The P.M.R.C. and Tipper Gore gave *Be My Slave* loads of PR. Explain the impact the P.M.R.C. had on the album and Bitch in general.
BB: The P.M.R.C gave us some of our best and most wide-spread publicity. Tipper Gore would appear on news channels such as CNN

speaking on behalf of her cause and she always had a copy of *Be My Slave* prominently on display. The fact that they put the warning label on the album only served to increase record sales. They even read aloud lyrics from our song, "Gimme A Kiss" during the congressional hearings to get the warning labels implemented.

MT: Your next album, *The Bitch is Back*, didn't come out until 1987. What was the delay in the release?

BB: Challenges with our management at the time. They wanted to take us in a different direction, re-shape our image and re-tool our music. They also were advising us to hold off on releasing the next album and take our time recording it.

MT: *The Bitch is Back* became Bitch's best-selling album. How much of that was due to your exposure by the P.M.R.C.?

BB: I would say a fair amount. Bitch was getting quite a bit of publicity because of it at the time, so I am sure that it helped with our record sales.

Betsy, December 2011.
Toluca Lake, CA

MT: Then in 1988, you changed the band's name to Betsy, and released a self-titled album. What was the reason for the name change?

BB: We wanted to see if the name, Bitch, was holding us back commercially. These days, you hear the word "bitch" all of the time and it's not the taboo term it used to be. So the name change to "Betsy" was sort of an experiment. In the long run, it seemed to make no difference, so we returned to the original – and better – name of Bitch.

MT: The name change also brought a different sound from the band. What were your thoughts on the change of direction?

BB: *Betsy* is my absolute favorite album with the band. I like hard rock and I like metal, but I also like melody. One of my favorite bands is Cheap Trick. *Betsy* had a much more slick, polished sound. We also had some outside songwriting for that release. I liked my vocals on that album better than any other Bitch release. I liked the production, I liked the songs. It was a nice change of pace.

MT: Bitch's last release came out in 1989, *A Rose By Any Other Name*. It was an EP featuring a potpourri of remixes from the band. Why not release a full length album?
BB: We didn't have anything new recorded. We had a lot of odds and ends, remixes, and songs that we recorded that never made it onto a release. It was enough to put something out, so that is what we did. It was sort of an "interim" project.

MT: Although Bitch hasn't visited the studio in years, you still gig on occasion. In 2003, you played the Bang Your Head!!! Festival in Germany with some other big acts. What was that experience like?
BB: Definitely the best live experience Bitch ever had. It was great. The fans over there are awesome. They love their metal and are so appreciative. Our time slot was 11:30 in the morning on a Friday. I wasn't sure if I was going to be able to find my singing voice that early in the morning, but I was in really good form. The band played great. They had a huge stage with a runway that went out into the crowd. The promoters treated us like royalty, and everything was over the top. Getting to work with Dio, Twister Sister, Y&T, U.D.O., and others was such a great experience. The only thing bad about it was that we had to return home!

MT: How big was the crowd?
BB: Between 12,000-15,000 people. A sea of adoring metal fans as far as the eye could see.

MT: Through 2003, David Carruth, Robby Settles, and you were considered Bitch's original members. Why did David leave in 2003?
BB: He just didn't want to continue with the band anymore. I really don't know the actual reason. I should ask him sometime. But Robby and I re-formed with different players which included two guitarists instead of one.

MT: What do you think Bitch's challenge is with holding on to bass players?
BB: I don't know! It's them! Bass players are a weird bunch. Each one of our fifteen bass players - and I'm not exaggerating - always had

something different happen with them. Robby, David, and I were the core and we were always together. Well, David was my boyfriend, and Robby was my brother-in-law so it wasn't too hard. It's not like we ever made the bass player feel like an outsider, it was just always some different scenario with our revolving door of bass players. Ron Cordy was with us the longest, and also a great bass player and performer. When I think of Bitch's most important bass player, I think of him.

MT: How often was Bitch gigging between 2003 - 2009?
BB: Not too often. Robby and I had put the band back together with some new members. And I was filling in on lead vocals with a band called, "Witch", for a while. "Bitch" never really broke up. We just weren't playing on a regular basis – just kind of laying low.

MT: In early 2009, you learned that your friend/brother-in-law/drummer Robby Settles was diagnosed with leukemia. Was Robby the one to break the news to you?
BB: No, it was my sister.

MT: Robby passed in May 2010. What are some of your fondest memories of him?
BB: He was a great friend, a great brother-in-law, an awesome father to my nieces and an amazing husband to my sister. He was great fun to hang out with and was the perfect hard-hitting drummer for Bitch. After David and I split up, he acted as my advisor and mentor and sort of took on the role of taking care of me, as well as taking care of my sister and their three daughters. Some of the best years of my life were spent with him, in terms of both the band, and also my family life.

MT: Throughout the life of Bitch, you have always maintained or improved your physical appearance. How do you do it?
BB: I have always taken pride in my appearance. As the years progress, I make sure that I continue to eat healthy. I work out every other day and pretty much adhere to that schedule on a regular basis. I have had some cosmetic surgery. Nothing too radical, but in 2007, I had a facelift and had my eyes done. And, a year before that I got breast implants.

MT: Was that your first breast augmentation?
BB: Yes. I went from a 32A to a 34D. They are saline, and were put under the muscle.

MT: Do you cook?
BB: Yes, I am a really good cook!

MT: If you had to make one dish to impress somebody, what would it be?
BB: I make this really good rolled-up chicken breast. I make a stuffing of cheese, sautéed mushrooms, green onion, and spinach. I pound the chicken breast, put the stuffing in the middle, and roll it up. Then I roll that up into a crescent roll dough. I bake it, and then put hollandaise sauce over it when it's done. It's so good!

MT: How often are you recognized out in public?
BB: Quite a bit. Enough that it floors me when I go out some place. I never take it for granted, and I am always very appreciative of the fans. I always shake their hand and pose for photos if they ask.

Betsy in West Hollywood, March 2010.
Photo by Digital Pam.

MT: What is your adult drink of choice?
BB: I don't drink anymore. Not because I had a problem with alcohol, but I just didn't feel good the following day regardless of how little I drank. Just two beers would give me a migraine the next day. Back in the day I enjoyed champagne, or vodka and cranberry, but now I am afraid to even take a drink as I don't want to feel like that again.

MT: What kind of car do you drive?
BB: I just sold my classic 1971 Volkswagen Karmann Ghia that I loved. I had it for nearly twenty years. The transmission went out, and I wanted something with air conditioning and a CD player, so I bought a 1993 Honda Del Sol. It's a two-seater convertible, and candy apple red. I am really enjoying it.

186

MT: Do you smoke cigarettes?
BB: No. I used to smoke socially, but now I think it's a disgusting habit.

MT: When was your last brush with the law?
BB: I got nailed by one of those red light cameras, and it really pissed me off! (laughs). It is so freaking expensive. It was $424, and there is nothing that you can do to dispute it. The only silver lining was that the photo of me flying through the red light was really good!

MT: Who is the best musician you ever jammed with?
BB: I'd have to say Vinny Appice. My friend threw a party and Vinny was her drum teacher, so he came to the party. There were a lot of musicians there and we all started jamming. We weren't lacking for any instrument, everything was covered. Vinny was playing drums, and I was singing. I think we played, "Smoke on the Water".

MT: Where is your favorite place to hang out locally?
BB: There is a club I play at quite a bit called Paladino's. It's in the San Fernando Valley close to where I live. There is always a good band playing there, and I get in for free. I also play there quite a bit, both with Bitch, and a "just for fun" cover band I throw together with various musician friends called "Betsy Bitch & The Knockers". I still like to go to Hollywood, but it is a little more of a time investment and it's usually for something specific, like a band I'm seeing at House of Blues, or a guest list I'm on for The Roxy or The Whisky.

MT: What was your drug of choice back in the day?
BB: Marijuana. I never went any further than that.

MT: If you took a drug test today, what would it tell us?
BB: It would tell us that Betsy Bitch enjoys a hit of marijuana to relax every so often.

MT: Should marijuana be legalized?
BB: I think that it should be. It definitely has some healing qualities. I can see how it benefits cancer and AIDS patients as it promotes a good feeling and appetite. It's organic, and usually not cut with anything. It's not a drug that can kill you like heroin, meth, or cocaine.

MT: What is your wildest sexual experience?

BB: Well, a long time ago Robin Zander from Cheap Trick and I passionately made out, but we didn't actually do the deed. But it was a great experience gazing into his eyes and having a drink with him, then getting to kiss him at the end of the night. But as for my wildest experience, when I was younger I went out to dinner with a group of people at this restaurant. I found the bartender really attractive so when it came time to leave, I told my friends to go on without me, and I sat and talked with the bartender. It was his turn to close the restaurant that night, so I hung out with him. We ended up doing it on the floor of the closed restaurant. I got a nasty restaurant rug burn….

MT: Who do you listen to now? Who are you listening to in your car?

BB: I still love classic rock. Alice Cooper and Cheap Trick. I also really like The Darkness. But I still listen to Judas Priest, Iron Maiden, Whitesnake - even more mainstream stuff like Foreigner, Journey, Damn Yankees, etc. I still like all of the classic bands.

MT: Have you ever been afraid for your safety while on stage performing?

BB: Just once. We were playing The Roxy, and I got a little too close to the edge of the stage and got pulled into the crowd. And quite deep into the crowd. Two roadies had to jump into the audience to help me get back to the stage. I had never felt so many hands all over my body in my life.

MT: If you had a crystal ball, what age would it tell us you live to?

BB: I want to live forever. I don't ever see myself getting old. I want to say ninety, but that is still too young!

MT: While performing, have you ever called a venue or city by the wrong name?

BB: No. I am pretty mindful of where I am and who I am addressing.

MT: When you sing in the car or shower, is it typically your songs that you sing?

BB: No. Never.

MT: Who would make you star-struck?

BB: Alice Cooper, who I have met a few times, but I can never meet him enough times.

MT: When was the last time you were blown away by a band's live performance?

BB: Just a couple nights ago when I saw "The Darkness" at House of Blues.

MT: What do you look for in a guy when dating?

BB: Well, looks at first. Rock'n'roll looks. I am partial to long-haired rockers. But that always gets me in trouble because they end up being assholes. It would be nice if they weren't assholes and were good looking, and had a sense of humor, and had integrity, and had money. (laughs).

MT: What advice would you provide to a player who wants to play rock music for a living?

BB: Make sure you do what you do well before you embark on it. Develop your talent. Back that talent up with charisma, and make sure you look good while you're doing it. Be interesting to your audience, and pull them in. Don't be a poser, and don't be cliché. Make sure the audience knows that you're enjoying what you're doing, and let them in on the fun.

MT: What are you working on now? How can people get a hold of you?

BB: There is www.betsybitch.com which was started by a fan, David Gaston, who has become a friend. It's pretty thorough and up-to-date. I have a Facebook page under Betsy Weiss. I was recently in the studio singing a duet with Steve Gaines for the upcoming Anger As Art release. A song called Rage and Retribution. Anger As Art is the band that became "Bitch" on our recent European tour. My cover band, Betsy Bitch & the Knockers, are still gigging occasionally. Bitch is hoping for some European festival opportunities this summer, but more to follow on that. We're headlining an all-metal night at the world famous, Whisky a Go Go, on the Sunset Strip in May, which will be the first time we've played that particular venue in over 20 years. I intend to keep Bitch going in some way, shape or form as long as the fans are out there, and as long as journalists are interested in interviewing me. Thanks for everyone's support.

Ron Keel promo photo, 2010. Photo by Alex Solca.

Ron Keel

Lead Vocals/Guitar

Past- Steeler, Iron Horse, Fair Game, Saber Tiger

Present- Keel, Country Super Star Show, Solo

MT: When is your birthday?
RK: March 25, 1961.

MT: The city you were raised in?
RK: Too many to mention, but Phoenix, Arizona more so than any other.

MT: The city you currently reside?
RK: Las Vegas, Nevada.

MT: Did you graduate high school?
RK: No.

MT: Marital Status?
RK: Married.

MT: Any kids?
RK: Two. Kelly is 27, and Ryan is 24.

MT: When did you first realize that you enjoyed music?
RK: I believe it was February 1964 when I saw The Beatles on the Ed Sullivan Show.

MT: Were you active in singing groups in school?
RK: Yes. It's all I have ever done. Basically, I was in my first band in 5th grade. By the time I got into high school I had a pierced ear, long hair, wearing leather, getting laid, and playing gigs. I was playing clubs when I was 14. I was 6'2" or 6'3" and looked a lot older than I was. I was hanging out with guys who were a lot older than me, and the drinking age was 18 at the time. So yeah, I was playing clubs at 14.

MT: After high school, you performed in a couple Nashville-based bands, "Lust" then "Steeler". Do you recall the conversation in Nashville when the band decided to relocate to LA in the early 80s?
RK: Yes, in 1981 the band and the guitarist's family had a meeting to discuss the move. Our guitarist's family had a lot of money and they wanted to invest in the band. I had come to the conclusion that if we're going to make a move, I had to get the band to LA. I kind of predicted that LA was where the heavy metal surge was going to happen before I had ever heard of Motley Crue or Ratt. Our choices were LA or New York. LA was the beach, Hollywood, girls - it was a dreamland. So, I made the decision to relocate the band to LA. Our guitar player's family invested enough money in the band to get us to LA and get started.

MT: Was your family supportive of the move?
RK: My family? My family probably didn't know anything about the move. I wasn't close with my parents at the time. They had pretty much given up hope on me when I left home, dropped out of high school, and went on the road with a rock'n'roll band. They thought my life was over. They didn't come around til I had a band called, "Keel." They thought I named the band after them. They saw me selling out shows, selling records, heard me on the radio, and saw me on TV. Then they started to realize that there might be something to this music thing.

MT: Shortly after you arrived in LA, you met Brian Slagel who was preparing to release an album of unreleased metal bands from LA called, *Metal Massacre*(MM)#1. How did you meet Brian?
RK: Brian was working at Oz Records. I believe that he contacted us, as we had started to make some noise on the scene. Our investors gave us enough money to get to LA and get started, but I told them that we needed a record. We needed some kind of tangible representation of our music. But, they would not finance it. But he did give us $100 each as a Christmas bonus. There were four guys in the band, and three in the crew. So with that $700, we made the "Cold Day in Hell" 45 single, which really got Steeler off the ground. That is when Brian Slagel and I started talking extensively, and we agreed to let him use that song on the first *Metal Massacre* album.

MT: The Steeler song, "Cold Day in Hell," appeared on the first pressing of MM #1? What affect did the album's release have on Steeler?

RK: We had released the song and 45 prior to Metal Massacre's release to rave reviews. I don't know the exact impact that Metal Massacre had on our career, but it was a ground breaking record.

MT: Due to the unexpected popularity of MM#1, a second pressing of MM#1 took place shortly after the first. "Cold Day in Hell" was replaced by "Chains Around Heaven" by Black 'n Blue on the second pressing. Why was that?
RK: That was my agreement with Brian. I'm not sure that it was a good call at the time, or a good decision on our part. I was still learning the business. It was probably a mistake, but I was just trying to take care of our business. There is no way of knowing, but when you're 21 years old managing a band by yourself in LA, I thought it was the right call at the time. It was probably stupid.

Ron performing with Steeler at The Whisky in Hollywood, 1982. Photo from the private collection of Ron Keel.

MT: Steeler then went through wholesale personnel changes adding Rik Fox, Mark Edwards, and an unknown guitarist, Yngwie Malmsteen. Do you remember your first conversation with Yngwie? How did it go?
RK: I do remember our first conversation. He said he was a team player, he loved the Steeler music, wanted to come to come to America, and wanted to be in a band with me. He said all of the right things and convinced me that it was the right decision to bring him to America and cut that record with him.

MT: Once Yngwie joined Steeler, did the band head right into the studio?

RK: No. We went right into rehearsal. The first day, I realized that Yngwie's style and mine were not compatible. So, I made him sit on the couch for a few days while we auditioned other guitarists. After three days of listening to all these other guitar players auditioning for his gig, and realizing that he was going home to Sweden, he came to me and said, "I know what you want. I want to do this. I can do this," and of course he could do it. He could play anything he wanted to play. So, he came into rehearsal and played the songs with an American heavy metal style, and that's when I decided that we could make it work. We did nine gigs, played together for four months, and recorded that ground breaking *Steeler* album, which was Yngwie's first album as well as mine.

MT: One would assume that having Yngwie Malmsteen in your band would be a positive thing. Would you say that was true?

RK: It was positive because the record is a milestone of that era. It was an interesting combination of my songs, and my style with Yngwie's guitar playing. It could have been more positive for both of us if we hadn't been so young and stubborn. We both made some mistakes, and we have to live with the results of those mistakes.

MT: Steeler released their self-titled album, *Steeler*, in 1983. How was the band getting along at the time the album was released?

RK: The day the album came out there were no members in the band that actually played on the album. I did a record signing at Tower Records in LA that day, and there were three other guys in the band. Yngwie, Rik, and Mark were gone. The band was getting along great, but they weren't the same guys that played on the record.

MT: What was the reason for the line-up changes?

RK: Yngwie left to join Alcatrazz. At the time, it was a very amicable parting. Yngwie was heavily influenced by Ritchie Blackmore and even if we had been getting along as best buddies, when Graham Bonnet called he would have been gone. Obviously, with Yngwie gone, we needed to make a change at bass as well. So Rik Fox and I parted ways. We added Mitch Perry on lead guitar, and Ron Murray on bass.

MT: How much did Steeler tour in support of the album, and who did you share a bill with?

RK: We did not tour at the time. We were trying to get a major record deal. We opened for Motley Crue. We played with Y&T a lot. Our manager was Y&T's booking agent. We were basically headlining making $2,000-$3,000 a night at venues throughout California.

MT: Steeler eventually disbanded in 1984, and your solo project, Keel, was formed. At what point did you know that was the direction you were headed?

RK: There was a time in early 1984 that I realized Steeler - even though it had been my baby, my dream, my vision - I had to let it go in order to succeed. My goal was to put the ultimate commercial hard rock, heavy metal band in LA together, and get a major record deal. I realized that wasn't going to happen with Steeler because of the instability of the line-up changes. I decided to put together Keel based on me, my songs, my voice, and my vision. I put together Keel in March of 1984. Strangely enough, like you mentioned, it was started as somewhat of a solo project and it ended up being a real band. It was a family. A group of guys that really loved and cared about each other, that worked hard to achieve the same goals, and still are almost 30 years later. Four out of five of those guys are still with me to this day.

MT: With Keel you brought together a group of incredibly talented musicians, including Marc Ferrari. How did you meet Marc?

RK: Mike Varney had given Marc my number. I came home one day and checked the phone messages that my girlfriend had taken for me. The note pad read; "Marc Ferrari called. Call Marc Ferrari. Marc Ferrari called again." It was literally a full page of messages from him. He was relentless. I thought he had a pretty cool name, and I called him back. He said that he played lead guitar and was interested in joining my band. I went to pick him up in Hollywood. He didn't even have a car at the time - now he has quite a collection of them. But, he was ready to go to work. He had a relentless work ethic. He was a good looking kid, and played a great, melodic guitar. He was a godsend. He was ready to succeed at any cost.

MT: Marc has mentioned that you ran your rehearsals for Keel very structured and regimented, like a musical boot camp. Is that a fair assessment?

RK: That is putting it mildly. My work ethic is, get to work early, stay late, and bust your ass while you're there. We were on a mission. I had made a promise to the guys in Keel. I asked them to give me three months. I told them that, "In three months we will be making a record, we'll be playing to thousands of people, we'll be on the radio and doing stuff we have never done before, just trust me. Do what I say. Let's go to work." It was very competitive. Everyone was getting a record deal, and we wanted one too. I thought if we worked harder than everyone else, it just might happen. And it did.

MT: Around this time, you had also met with Tony Iommi and Geezer Butler from Black Sabbath. Is it true that Tony told you that you had the gig of Lead Vocalist for Black Sabbath during the very early stages of Keel?
RK: That is correct. Tony, Geezer, Don Arden, and Spencer Proffer who was going to produce their album and I had an understanding. I was told that I was the singer in Black Sabbath, and I have a contract that states that as well. I was actually in the band for a few days.

MT: You even called a meeting with the members of Keel telling them you were joining Black Sabbath, correct?
RK: That is correct, yes.

MT: What ended up happening with the Black Sabbath gig?
RK: My deal was with Spencer Proffer. He had produced the first Quiet Riot album that sold 10 million copies, and he was the hot hand in LA. Spencer had heard me on the Keel demos, and tagged me for the gig with Black Sabbath because he was set to produce the new Sabbath record, the follow-up to *Born Again*. I was to replace Ian Gillan, and I had done a demo of songs that Spencer was trying to get Sabbath to record. He was trying to turn them into an 80s metal hair band. Sabbath wasn't having any of that, and I certainly agreed with them. Sabbath had to be true to their roots. Spencer ended up getting fired, and I got caught in the crossfire.

MT: Keel's first album, *Lay Down the Law*, came out in 1984. About this time, you had just become a parent for the first time. Was it a struggle to combine the responsibilities of parenthood and rock stardom?
RK: It always is. Being a parent and having a job are going to conflict, it doesn't matter what the job is. There are going to be times when the kids need you, and you can't be there. Anyone that's a parent certainly understands the struggle of dividing your time as a professional, and trying to give your kids the time and attention they deserve.

MT: The album received rave reviews, and even impressed Gene Simmons. How long after the album was released were you contacted by Gene?

RK: We were actually contacted by Gene before the record was finished, and *Lay Down the Law* is not what got Gene's attention. We were still mixing the record when I got a call from my manager. He had set up some showcases in LA, and had some major label interest. So, the band came back to LA during the sessions, showcased for a number of record labels, and ended up signing with Gold Mountain, because they wanted us the most. They believed in what we were doing, and signed the band pretty much overnight. They gave me a list of potential producers for the next album. There were a lot of hot names on the list, but I wanted Gene Simmons. I told them to hook me up with him. I met Gene at The Beverly Hills Hotel, and went up to his room. During the *Lay Down the Law* sessions, we had recorded a rough recording of "The Right to Rock," the song. Ferrari had launched into that riff out of nowhere, and I yelled to the engineer, "Hit record." So I had that rough recording with me when I met with Gene. There is no vocal on the recording, but I slapped it in a boom box and sang, "The Right to Rock" face to face, literally spitting in his face! He leaned over and hit stop on the boom box, and said, "I'm going to produce this record. And we're going to start Tuesday." That was before *Lay Down the Law* was finished, or released.

MT: Keel went into the studio with Gene Simmons to record, "The Right to Rock." How often was Gene present?

RK: Gene was present during every session. We didn't work without him. During the LA sessions we did basic tracks, background vocals, rhythm guitars, but then he had to go on tour with Kiss. So we relocated to New York to finish the sessions, and had to work around Gene's schedule. He would fly into New York for a few hours, or a day and we would track. He would then leave to do some Kiss shows, and we would have a day or two or three to get into trouble. When Gene was available, we would record. When he was on tour with Kiss, we would party our brains out!

MT: Did you ever second guess your decision to bring Gene aboard?

RK: Absolutely not. Not then, not now.

MT: How did you feel about having to use three of Gene's songs on the album?

RK: I thought it was amazing. I grew up singing Gene Simmons songs. All of my bands when I was a kid played Kiss tunes. To be able to be friends with him, and have him as a mentor, and have him on our team and in our family was a huge blessing. We included the three Gene songs because things happened so quickly. As I said, we were still recording *Lay Down the Law* when we got the deal. We wanted a January of 1985 release date. We had to work around Gene's Kiss schedule. We didn't have enough new songs. I literally stayed up all night and wrote, "The Right to Rock," "Back to the City," and "Electric Love" in the same night. Those were the three new songs on the album. We re-recorded three songs from *Lay Down the Law*. And then using three of Gene's songs, we had enough material for the "The Right to Rock." This way we could start recording on Tuesday like Gene wanted to.

MT: Do you recall how the publishing was split on those three songs?

RK: Those were Gene's. We didn't get any publishing on those.

MT: *The Right To Rock* included the single by the same name, and became your most successful album to date, selling just under 500,000 units. Do you recall how big your bonus would have been if the album would have been certified Gold?

RK: It would have been considerable. If the record would have been certified Gold, it would have been a large chunk of change. We are of the belief that it is certainly a Gold record, and we have spent some time and money trying to prove that. But 30 years ago everything wasn't computerized, and unfortunately a lot of stuff got shoved under the table. Basically, we probably got screwed. But as far as I am concerned, it's a Gold record.

MT: After touring, Keel went right back into the studio with Gene and recorded *The Final Frontier*. The album got as high as #52 on The Billboard 200. Were you splurging with your money at all?

RK: I was not splurging. The expenses were extremely high at the time. Our nut for touring was $16,000 a week for the band, the crew, and the bus. We were subsidized by our publishing advances and merchandising. We did not see a whole lot of money. I got a huge tax bill that year, but the money wasn't going into my pocket.

MT: The album, *Keel,* was released in 1987 with Michael Wagener producing rather than Gene. What brought on this change?

RK: We had experienced huge momentum with *The Final Frontier*, which was an epic record. We did an extensive tour of Europe with Dio, but we did not have a whole lot of U.S. arena dates, ever. I think that there were two factors that did not allow us to succeed at the level we hoped for. One was that we never had a second single, except "Tears of Fire" from *The Final Frontier* album. The other was that we never had a major arena tour in the U.S. We were scheduled to tour with Metallica, but James Hetfield fell off of a skate board and broke his hand and the tour was cancelled. Yes, we toured with Motley Crue, for two dates. We toured with Bon Jovi for 14 dates. Cinderella had what - 300 dates on the *Slippery When Wet* tour? If the team isn't winning, you have to change the coach. Gene had come to us and wanted to dictate that the next album would contain 90% sexual content. I wanted to write songs that expressed my views, and it wasn't all about sex, drugs, and rock'n'roll at the time. So we parted ways with Gene, to work with Wagener, who made a great sounding record. That '87 self-titled record sonically competes with anything in the business, and still sounds great today.

MT: An unreleased track from the album, *Proud To Be Loud*, would eventually wind up on Pantera's *Power Metal* album, which Marc Ferrari produced early in 1988. Did Marc discuss this with you prior to Pantera's album being released?

RK: No, that was Marc's song. He could do with it what he liked. "Proud to be Loud" was not an unreleased track from the '87 album. It was actually a song that was in the running that we never cut.

MT: *Larger than Live* was released in 1989, and included a mixture of live and new studio material. After a strong five-year run, could you see the end was near for the band?

RK: Yes, I could. Being realistic, you always want to think that you have a fighting chance. But as soon as MTV said that they wouldn't play the video, we were dead. You needed to have three things back then, and you kind of still do. You need air play, you need a video on TV, and you have to have a tour. If you don't have all three of those things, you are pissing up a tree. It was obvious that we weren't going to get the video play on MTV. So, it was time to move on, and I put my band, Fair Game, together at that time.

MT: Keel disbanded in 1989, and Fair Game was formed. Your band mates were four beautiful women who could really play. Why do you think that project didn't have more longevity?

RK: Our genre, at the time was dead in the water. The entire genre. We all hit the ground hard. Some of us survived the fall, some of us didn't. During the 80s, we all thought our run was going to last forever. We went from being the heroes, to the laughing stock of the entertainment genre by 1990. It was literally Spinal Tap on steroids. At that time, no one was getting a record deal.

MT: After Fair Game your musical vision shifted. Tell us about that.

RK: Once Fair Game didn't get a deal - and we pushed it hard for three years - I realized that it was time for me to reassess my life and career. I pretty much lost everything. I went through a personal tragedy with my family, and it was a rough period. I relocated my family back to Arizona, and started a career in country music. I literally had nothing, and went back to my roots. I sat down with a guitar in front of a campfire in the desert and started writing country music. Country songs poured out of me. It was a way to express myself and a way to keep performing. It basically saved my life in 1992.

MT: You then joined Japan-based, Saber Tiger. As legend has it, you said you would do the project for $75,000. After you had a few cocktails, you were called back with a counter offer of $30,000 that you accepted. Was that how it went down?

RK: Yes, that's how it went down. I played in a honky-tonk that night, and was making $50 a gig for a six-hour set. It was brutal. After the gig, you would have a few drinks. When I got home, there was a fax on my desk from Fandango Records in Japan. They wanted me to call them regarding singing on the Saber Tiger project. They asked what I would charge to "make contract." I told them $75 grand. They said, "We call you back." So I had a couple more cocktails, and they called back five minutes later. They said "We give you $30,000 dollars." I said, "I'm there."

MT: You formed Iron Horse in 2000 which combined country and hard rock. You also perform in a lead role for the "The Country Superstars Tribute" show here in Las Vegas. Have you gotten any push back from your die-hard fans that prefer your heavier material?

RK: Yes, I have caught a lot of flack for it. A lot of people say, "Hey, you went country," or "Oh, you're back to singing metal again." I don't subscribe to those musical prejudices. When I was growing up, you could hear Black Sabbath and the Eagles on the same radio station. I love music, I love the ability to express myself, and that is what "The Right to Rock" is all about in the first place, god damn it! I am fighting for the freedom to express myself however I choose. That's what "The Right to Rock" is. If the fans don't get that, then they don't get "The Right to Rock" because that is what it is all about.

MT: How do you feel the last night of a long tour?
RK: On the last night of a major tour there is a lot of emotion, and a feeling of accomplishment. It doesn't really hit you til you get home, and if you don't dive right into something else, you will get post-tour depression. But, I have never experienced that. I am always on to the next challenge, or the next project, or the next show.

MT: If you were asked to do MTV's Cribs, would you do it?
RK: Sure. They are welcome anytime.

MT: How big is your current place you call home?
RK: It's probably 1500 square feet. I do have 10 beautiful acres in the Sierra Nevada Mountains, with a year-round trout stream running through it. That is really where I put my money and my heart. That's where I will end up some day. That is home. This is where I work.

MT: What kind of car do you own?
RK: I have a black, 2012 ProX 4x4 Nissan pick-up truck, which is absolutely amazing. I have nearly 3,000 miles on, and it is now marked with a number of "Nevada Pinstripes" from the trees and brush on the dirt roads.

MT: Are you registered to vote? Will you be voting in November (2012)? Who for?
RK: Absolutely, I am registered to vote. I do believe the vote is fixed, and I believe that our votes do not count. But, I will be voting. If I had the option, I would vote for Ron Paul.

MT: How often do you listen to your material from the 80s?
RK: Usually just when I am rehearsing for Keel shows. But if I'm going to just listen to Keel, I will listen to the new record, *Streets of Rock & Roll*.

MT: Do you smoke cigarettes? How many a day?
RK: I do. It depends on the day, as I only smoke when I sing. Like today, I will not smoke because I am not singing today. But if I quit smoking, my voice goes out the window. My pitch and my tone go right out the door.

MT: What was your drug of choice back in the day?
RK: Well, I was a pothead for most of my life. I enjoyed cocaine throughout the 80s and 90s as well. But, I have been drug-free now for five years. I couldn't imagine the effect drugs would have on me at this age. I was never over the top with it, and I never saw heroin. You hear all of this talk from Motley Crue and these guys, how they were junkies, but I am not really totally believing that. I knew those guys, and Nikki Sixx is a sharp businessman. Every time that I saw them, or played with them they didn't not seem like they were on drugs.

MT: Should marijuana be legalized?
RK: Yes. It probably should be.

Ron performing on the Monsters of Rock Cruise, February 2012. Photo by Renee Keel.

MT: Do you follow sports?
RK: I am an NFL junkie. I have been too much of a nomad all my life to be geographically rooted to one particular team. I was a huge John Elway fan, and I have retained my fan status with the Denver Broncos. I am a big fan of the Detroit Lions, because their coach, Jim Schwartz, is a Keel fan. He always "tweets" the music that they are listening to before the game. Every now and then he will tweet, "Listening to Keel." But, mostly I just enjoy the team aspect of it. I use a lot of football analogies in my

business. They put a bunch of guys together, and work their asses off to achieve a common goal, which is victory. That is basically how I run my business, and my bands.

MT: Craziest groupie story?
RK: The craziest ones are the guys who follow you around, pick up your cigarette butts and put them in a plastic baggie. The chicks don't bother me so much, but the male groupies will sometimes get a little scary. Of course, there were a lot of crazy times back in the day with chicks handcuffing themselves to the bus, and doing all kinds of nasty things. But, I was usually the guy who would give the girl $20, and send her home in a cab. I caught a lot of flak for that back in the day, but once I became a father it wasn't funny anymore. This was someone's little girl. When I started mentioning that in interviews, the shit hit the fan. People don't want that. They want the debauchery, the dirt, the heroin addict, and that's not me. That's my craziest groupie story. Giving a girl $20 and sending her home in a cab. Now *that's* crazy!

MT: What beverage do you drink during a show?
RK: It depends on the show. I typically have a couple shots of Jim Beam to loosen up. Then I will have a beer or two on stage to keep the whistle wet.

MT: What advice would you provide someone who wants to play rock music for a living?
RK: Do something else! I have been really blessed doing this. I make more money now than I ever have, but not everybody can do what I do. I have a 30-year track record to fall back on, and I am very diverse. I do solo/acoustic gigs, Las Vegas Stripped, Keel gigs, I write songs for TV and film, I give vocal lessons, I do recording sessions, the Country Tribute Show which I star in. I do a plethora of different things which enables me to make a living. But music is becoming like farming. When you have to pay $6,000 to make $3,000, you're in big trouble. There are too many ways of getting free music now. Why pay for it when you can get it for free? Bands starting out now play for free, or even pay to play. If you can make money performing as an up-and-coming artist, I applaud you.

MT: Keel reunited for their 25th Anniversary in 2008, and continues to gig. A big topic of discussion is a potential Steeler reunion for their 30th Anniversary. Will this happen, and if so, what Steeler line-up is the most likely to partake?

RK: I would like to do something special to celebrate Steeler's 30th anniversary. As far as reuniting with Yngwie, I would be willing to do that for historical purposes and to come full circle in our careers. I don't think that he's going to be willing to do that. You might want to ask him. I would bury the hatchet in a heartbeat to do something together. It would be cool and fun, and the fans would dig it. Why not?

MT: Would you consider doing a Steeler reunion without Yngwie?

RK: I think we'll have to wait and see. I'm trying to do something special to commemorate the 30th Anniversary of that release, and if I can do it right, we'll do it.

MT: What are you working on now? How can people get a hold of you?

RK: You can find me at www.ronkeel.com - that is my home on the internet. I have seen things like Myspace and Facebook come and go, but I am a firm believer in having the traditional, kick-ass website where fans can get on my Message Board or Forum and have one-on-one conversations with me. They can view my videos, listen to my music, they can see photo galleries throughout my career. I am still very active with Keel, and we are confirming tour dates for the rest of 2012. I'm looking forward to keeping the Country Tribute Show going as long as we can in Las Vegas. We have been running for five years now. I have a solo project in the works that is along the lines of the Iron Horse material. Kind of, 'Metal Cowboy,' if you will. Also, I am enjoying my new radio show which we have just gotten off the ground. We're now on 13 stations/networks worldwide, including FM/AM broadcast stations and the biggest internet station in Japan It's called the "Streets of Rock & Roll Radio Show" which I am producing and hosting. You can find that at ronkeel.com as well.

Brian in December 2002.
Photo courtesy of Metal Blade Records.

Brian Slagel

Chairman/CEO of Metal Blade Records

Los Angeles, California

MT: When is your birthday?
BS: February 14th.

MT: The city you were raised in?
BS: Woodland Hills, California.

MT: The city you currently reside?
BS: Los Angeles, California.

MT: Marital status?
BS: Single.

MT: Any children?
BS: No.

MT: Did you graduate high school?
BS: Yes. 1979.

MT: Do you play a musical instrument?
BS: No.

MT: Your first real experience in the music industry was working at Oz Records. How old were you when you started working there?
BS: I was 19.

MT: Originally, what was your role there?
BS: When I started I was a counter person. Just a regular employee.

MT: Rumor has it that you were a "Bootlegger" at the time. What is the coolest Bootleg you had back then?
BS: That is a tough question to answer as I had so many. I have to pick one of the ones that I recorded myself. (laughs). Probably AC/DC with Bon Scott at the Long Beach Arena back in 1979.

MT: How did you sneak the recorder in?
BS: That's a funny story. (laughs). I was talking to some friends about this the other day. You go to concerts now and everyone tapes the show with their cell phone, and nobody cares. Back then it was really difficult to tape the shows. I would sneak in the tape recorder under by belt, between my belt and pants. That way when they patted me down, they usually couldn't feel anything. But somehow I got caught a couple times. So then, I would have a buddy sneak batteries in with him. So if they caught me, I would say to Security, "Look, I parked far away. Just take the batteries." And then I would use the batteries that my buddy snuck in! (laughs).

MT: When you were working at Oz, do you remember what you were paid?
BS: I don't. I do remember it wasn't much, that's for sure.

MT: While you worked at Oz, you had several irons in the fire. When did you start producing your fanzine, "The New Heavy Metal Revue"?
BS: It was started in 1981.

MT: Who paid for the production of the fanzine? Was it a free publication?
BS: I did, and my buddy John threw in some money. We charged $1 for it.

MT: And you were also a correspondent for "Kerrang!" Paid gig?
BS: Yes. (laughs). It was supposed to be, and I eventually did get paid!

MT: Who were some of your friends back in the day that would visit you regularly at Oz?
BS: Jake E. Lee used to come in. Vince Neil came in a few times. Jay Reynolds. Lars as well.

MT: Jay Reynolds told us that he used to write for "The New Heavy Metal Revue". How was Jay to work with?
BS: Jay was great! Back then anyone who would write something for free, we were very happy to have! (laughs). But, Jay was cool. Jay was into Metal. He was awesome.

MT: You eventually talked the owners of Oz into carrying imports. How did you know where to find imports back then?

BS: Prior to working at the store, John, Lars and I would search southern California, as they were very hard to find. We would literally ask the people at the record store where they got their imports from. Also, before I began working at Oz, I was buying a lot of stuff from England and they told me there were some "Importers" over here. So at the time there was "Greenworld" in Los Angeles. In New York, there was "Import-ant"- they turned into Relitivity, and now R.E.D.

MT: And the imports sold well?
BS: Yes, they did huge business.

MT: Given your access to rare imports, did you experience a "Record Groupie" or two?
BS: No, unfortunately. (laughs). Back then it was 99% guys. Scratch that, it was 100% guys, and the only girls that would come in would be a couple of the guy's girlfriends.

MT: At what point did you decide that you wanted to do *Metal Massacre* #1 (MM1). What was the concept behind the album?
BS: I had been working at Oz for about six months. I noticed that Motley Crue and Ratt would play at the Troubadour for a dollar admission on a Wednesday night, and no one cared. I was a big fan of the New Wave of British Heavy Metal (NWOBHM). There were a lot of independent compilation albums coming over from Europe that were turning people on to a lot of different bands. That is what the concept was based on. There were a lot of good bands playing in LA that nobody knew about. The only way to get them any exposure was to put together a compilation album.

MT: How did the financing work?
BS: I had worked at Sears for a while in a commissioned sales position selling typewriters and cameras. (laughs). So I had saved up a little money. It wasn't much. Then, I borrowed some money from one of my aunts who had a little money. We're talking about hundreds of dollars here. And my friend, John Kornarens, pitched in a couple hundred bucks. We scraped it all together, and barely had enough money to manufacture 2,500 records. I think at the time we paid $1.50 a record, so it was $4,000 at the most.

MT: Is this when the business permits and licenses were filled for the creation of Metal Blade Records?
BS: I don't think I did any of that stuff when the compilation came out. It was really just an extension of the magazine. I had no intentions of ever starting a record company. I was just doing it to help the bands out. If you look at the first compilation, it states on the cover "The New Heavy Metal Revue Presents…" There was no business *anything* at that point. Metal Blade was formed the following year.

MT: You established Metal Blade as a private company, correct?
BS: Yes. It still is private.

MT: Do you own 100% of the stock?
BS: Just about.

MT: Can you explain how a label such as Metal Blade is different than a label like Warner Music Group?
BS: If you are on an Independent label, such as Metal Blade, it's a little bit less corporate. You have complete access to the person who runs the label, which would be me. It's a lot more of a family vibe as well. Everyone who attends to the artist is 100% into the music. It's easier and more user-friendly for the artist if they are dealing with people who understand their music better than the major labels do.

MT: What prevents Lars from walking into your office tomorrow and saying Metallica wants to use Metal Blade as their label?
BS: It's funny you mention that as he has joked about that several times. (laughs). I don't know that there is anything to prevent that from happening. I think for a band like Metallica or Van Halen, at this point in time, they could go to a major label and say, "Look, you guys do all the work, distribute and promote the record, and give us all of the money." The record label would take a very small percentage. So, theoretically we could do the same thing with them if they wanted, but we would be almost like a middleman. Even though we have major distribution, those bands can go right to the label and get a better "deal" so to speak.

MT: Jay Reynolds told us that Malice really didn't exist until you told him that his band could be on the album. Did you know at the time that was the case?
BS: That was kind of the case for several of those bands. So yes, we were aware of that.

MT: MM1 featured Malice, Bitch, Steeler, Ratt, and most notably, an unknown Metallica as well as others. What did you think of James Hetfield's voice the first time you heard it?

BS: (laughs). I would have to say that I wasn't particularly a big fan of it.

MT: How well did you know Cliff Burton?

BS: I knew him very well. Cliff's band, Trauma, was on *Metal Massacre II*. When the Metallica guys were looking for a bass player, I told them that they needed to check Cliff out, as I thought he was incredible. When Trauma came back to LA, the Metallica guys went to see them and loved Cliff…and the rest, as they say, is history.

MT: You printed 2500 copies of MM1, with hopes of selling them all. How much did the album retail for?

BS: I don't remember, but whatever the retail price was for an album in 1982. I think it was $7.99.

MT: At what point did you realize MM1 was a success?

BS: Well, we sold the first pressing really fast. At that point, I was getting asked for more albums, and realized that the album had done better than I thought it would.

MT: How did the publishing work for each artist for MM1?

BS: I knew nothing about running a label at that point, so it was very minimal. At some point, we figured out that we had to pay the publishing. I think eventually it got sorted out by getting a distribution deal with Greenworld, and they ended up doing a lot of that work for me.

MT: If I wanted to buy a *Metal Massacre* #1 on eBay, what do they go for now?

BS: That's a good question. I'm not sure about eBay, but I have seen the original ones with the misspelling of Metallica (spelled "Mettallica" on the first pressing) at European festivals for $300.

MT: Was there an artist, or individual that drove you nuts during the first few *Metal Massacre* releases? Did anyone rub you the wrong way?

BS: No, no. Not at all.

MT: Really? No one?

BS: No, no one gave me any problems. I guess the only bummer was when Steeler dropped out after the first pressing. That's when Black 'n Blue went on the album.

MT: Why did Steeler drop out after the first pressing?

BS: When the first pressing came out, I really didn't know what I was doing. I didn't have any contracts or anything like that. Then when we did the second pressing, we had to get everybody under contract. At that point, the Steeler guys felt that they had gotten what they wanted out of it, and I guess they were ready to sign another deal. Motley Crue was supposed to be on the album as well, and they dropped out at the last second because they had their album coming out.

MT: Over the years you have put out many of *Metal Massacre* releases, the last one being XIII. You have featured Slayer, Armored Saint, Lizzy Borden, Fates Warning, Metal Church, and dozens of others. Is there an artist that you passed on, who went on to do big things?

BS: I don't know that we ever passed on anyone from a *Metal Massacre* standpoint that went on to do big things. The two bands that were supposed to be on the album, that ended up not being were Motley Crue, and Mercyful Fate. They were in a similar situation as Motley, where they had a record deal with a company in Holland and didn't want to put a track on the record because they had that deal. Those are the two bands that I would have loved to have on the album, but weren't.

MT: Do you know what song of Motley's would have been on the album?

BS: I'm trying to remember if it was recorded or not. I know that they had a demo at that point. I had done a lot of work with their managers. In fact, they would come to my mom's house and we would meet on my mom's couch. I remember them saying one time, "We have 1500 Motley Crue records that we printed up. What do we do with them?" I said, "Why don't you take them to the distributor I know, Greenworld?" (laughs). If I only knew then what I know now!

MT: In 1984, Dave Mustaine's new band, Megadeth, was looking for a record label, and ended up signing with Combat Records. Having known him from Metallica, did you talk to Dave about signing with Metal Blade?

BS: Absolutely. He wrote me a really nice, long letter back in the time of letters. I wish I had it. It was between us and Combat. This was back in the day when no one had any money. We offered $8,000 and Combat offered $9,000. So they went with Combat for the extra $1,000.

MT: It seems Metal Blade has steered away from the compilation albums as of late, and focusing more on individual band releases. Is that fair to say?
BS: Yes. The compilations were really there to turn people on to new bands. Now with the internet, Myspace, and all of the other ways to hear bands, there really isn't a need for someone to put out a compilation record for people to check out bands.

MT: If you had to pick Metal Blades current "crown jewel", who would it be?
BS: That's a tough one. Probably Cannibal Corpse.

MT: Metal Blade has blown up in the last 10 years to be much more than a record label. How do you describe what Metal Blade does to people unfamiliar with your company?
BS: As the music industry has changed, we have become more of a service company than a record label. We still do a lot of things that record labels do, but we focus a lot on marketing, promotion, and branding. We just don't look at a band and say, "we have to sell their records." We look at the whole package. Branding and social media are super important now, and we work with the bands to grow them in all of these mediums. The bigger the band gets in general, the more CDs we're going to sell. So, if the band is huge in all of these areas, our CD sales will do well. So we partner with the bands. We're actually more of a service company than anything else.

MT: You have done many interviews for Metal Blade TV. Who has been your favorite?
BS: There are a couple. One of my favorites is the one I did with the Arch/Matheos guys. I am a huge John Arch fan. He has been in hibernation so long, and to be able to have him come in and talk with him was cool. There is also a recent one that we did with my friends Jim Florentine and Don Jamieson. That was fun for me just because those guys are a riot!

MT: How many people are currently on Metal Blades payroll?
BS: I think we have 23 now.

MT: It appears that you are still friends with the Metallica guys. How cool was it attending their Rock and Roll Hall of Fame Induction Ceremony as their guest?

BS: That was amazing. Those sorts of things are just crazy! Then you have the moment with them later in the evening after a few beverages, and you just look at each other and say, "How the hell did this all happen?" Especially with those guys, it's always so surreal because I have known them for so long, especially Lars. You have those few moments where you sit down and say, "How did this go from being kids listening to music in a bedroom to this?" The Rock and Roll Hall of Fame was one of those watershed moments.

Brian talking with media during New England Metal and Hardcore Festival, Worcester MA. April 2007. Photo courtesy of Metal Blade Records.

MT: Do you ever sit back and reflect on the role you played in helping develop the metal movement in the US?

BS: Not really. I mean, people will mention it to me, but I am just a fan. If I played a role that made a lot of people listen to metal, that's cool. But I am really just a fan.

MT: Was there a band early on that you though would be huge, but never got out of first gear?
BS: There is a band called, Little Caesar, that we did an EP with in the mid 80s. They came out right after Guns N Roses, and had that same type of sound. They had a metal, blues type genre to them. They were phenomenal live, and just a phenomenal band. Everybody thought that they were going to be huge, so we did the EP to set things up. Then they signed with Geffen and it never happened.

MT: What is the craziest thing you have seen during a business meeting in your career?
BS: (laughs). I was in Italy in the mid 90s, and I was meeting with a band called, Labyrinth, and their manager. They got so drunk that they got into a huge fight while we were trying to have this meeting.

MT: If you were asked to do MTV's Crib's, would you do it?
BS: Sure, why not?

MT: How big is your current home?
BS: The biggest one I have is in the desert in California which is about 2600 square feet. Everything else is like a condo which is at, or near, water.

MT: What kind of car do you drive?
BS: A 2010 white, Toyota Prius.

MT: Do you own any stocks? If so, which ones?
BS: Yes, but not a lot. Whole Foods, Apple, Trader Joe's, and the Central Hockey League. But not much of any of them.

MT: Are you registered to vote? Will you be voting in November (2012)? Who for?
BS: Yes and yes. I don't know yet. I am undecided.

MT: Rumor has it that you love Hockey?
BS: Yes. Growing up as a kid I was a huge fan of all sports, and went to a lot of hockey games, and started to get more into that sport. I love all sports though.

MT: Do you have any tattoos?
BS: No.

MT: Do you smoke cigarettes?
BS: No.

MT: Where is your favorite public place to hang out?
BS: I would say the Council Oak Lounge at the Hard Rock in Tampa, Florida. Locally, I would say the Geisha House.

MT: What was your drug of choice back in the day?
BS: I really never did drugs.

MT: Should marijuana be legalized?
BS: Yes.

MT: Of all the clubs on the Sunset Strip, which is your favorite and why?
BS: The Roxy. I love the layout of the room visually, and it sounds great sonically.

MT: When was the last run in with the law?
BS: Outside of a speeding ticket four years ago, I have never had one.

MT: Who is the one person that you run into knowing you're going to have a long night of partying ahead of you?
BS: Lars Ulrich.

MT: When was the last time you were blown away by a band's live performance?
BS: I'd have to say the last time I saw Rammstein. They are from Germany and have been around for a long time. They only sing in German, and they have this unbelievable stage show. I would say they put on the biggest and best stage show that I have ever seen in my life. Just phenomenal!

MT What is the best rock album ever produced?
BS: Iron Maiden, *The Number of the Beast*.

MT: Professionally speaking, what are you most proud of?
BS: Probably the longevity of the label.

MT: What advice would you provide to someone interested in starting their own record label?
BS: Do it for the love of the music.

MT: What are you working on now? How can people get a hold of you?
BS: You can go to www.metalblade.com to see all of our latest updates. You can "Like" us or follow us on Facebook. You can follow us on Twitter @metalblade, and you can follow me on Twitter @brianslagel.

Brian at Vamp'd in Las Vegas appearing with The Zep Set.
April 2012. Photo by Harold Mountain.

Brian Tichy

Drums

Past: Ozzy, Lynch Mob, Slash's Snakepit, Billy Idol, Foreigner, Sass Jordan, Vinnie Moore, Pride & Glory

Present: Whitesnake, Something Unto Nothing (S.U.N., guitar), T&N

MT: When is your birthday?
BT: August 18th.

MT: Do you have a nick name?
BT: Tish.

MT: The city you were raised in?
BT: Parsippany, New Jersey.

MT: The city you currently reside?
BT: LA, California. Santa Clarita, to be exact.

MT: Did you graduate high school?
BT: Yes, in 1986.

MT: Marital status?
BT: Single

MT: Any kids?
BT: Two amazing daughters that are the center of my life.

MT: At what age did you realize that you were interested in playing drums?
BT: I was five. I thought that at the top of "Mt. Coolness" that there would be a drum set. I thought that drums were the coolest thing on the planet, and that everyone at age five wanted to play them, but not everybody gets that chance. Something just connected with me with the look and sound of a drum kit.

MT: Then at age 12 you started playing guitar?
BT: Yes, at 12 or 13. At the peak of "Mt. Coolness" next to the drums, there was a Les Paul! I have always loved the sound of a guitar. My dad had an acoustic guitar, and he showed me the riff to "Day Tripper". He showed me a G and an E chord. It hurt! You have to build up calluses like on the drums. After a couple years, I started picking up guitar licks from my buddies, and didn't stop.

MT: Like most young rock drummers at the time, is it safe to assume that Peter Criss and Neil Peart were major influences?
BT: Yes, I think if they weren't at that time, something was really wrong with you. Peter Criss "100,000 Years" drum solo off of *Kiss Alive*, one of the coolest ever. Right next to that, Neil Peart, live "YYZ" off of *Exit...Stage Left*. To me that is Neil Peart peaking.

MT: Were your parents supportive of your interest in music?
BT: 100 percent.

MT: Did you play percussion in your high school band?
BT: Lead snare drum, Bro! (laughs). I think we were playing on Ludwig 6 ½ x 14 Super Sensitive's, as I remember the crisp, clean sound of a snare drum in a music room.

MT: Rather than attend a traditional college, you chose to attend the Berklee College of Music. Who did you hang out with while at Berklee?
BT: Some of my best friends at the time, and my buddies still are JD. John Deservio, the bass player for Black Label society - he is Uncle JD to my kids. Dorian Heartsong and Allen Pahanish were the rhythm section of Powerman 5000. We all played together in bands, lived together in dorms, we learned from each other, and we're all still buds.

MT: In 1991 and 1992, you toured with Vinnie Moore. What were your thoughts when you heard that Vinnie would be opening for Rush for 10 dates on the tour?
BT: I think collectively, we all nearly passed out! We were beyond stoked. We were all traveling in a van in upstate New York in December, playing clubs six nights a week. It was freezing. To get an opportunity like that was nothing short of complete insanity and an honor. To pull up in a van to Madison Square Garden, and set up my Tama Swingstars from high school on Neil's stage? In front of his drums? Are you kidding me?! To be able to sit there and talk with the

man, and have him ask if I would like to play his drums? Forget it, and that did happen at Madison Square Garden. That was one of the coolest highlights of all the things I've done.

MT: How often would you interact with Neil? What was he like?
BT: He was always super cool. He was endorsed by Zildjian cymbals at the time, and so was I, but Neil didn't know that. My contact with Zildjian, John DeChristopher, is proud to tell the story that around that time, Neil reached out to him and said, "You guys should check out this guy, Brian Tichy. He's really good." John got to reply, "Don't worry, Neil. We already have him."

MT: Shortly afterwards, you joined Pride & Glory with Zakk Wylde for an album and tour in 1993. Had you known Zakk prior?
BT: Yes, through my buddy, John Deservio. Zakk and I had jammed at clubs or clinics numerous times over the years, so he knew my drumming. When it came time to get a drummer for Pride & Glory, he just called me and asked, "What are you doing? Do you want to do this?"

MT: What do you remember most about that tour?
BT: Beer consumption! (laughs). I just remember that there was a lot of new stuff being discovered for me. I was in a band that was supporting a record that I actually came up with the drum parts, and played them the way I wanted. Zakk and James (Lomenzo, bass) gave me pretty much total freedom on that album. Having a record come out on Geffen, with major management, and knowing that you're going to be playing festivals in Europe, playing with Aerosmith, playing with Pantera, doing radio interviews, supporting a record that you are part of, is really special. I have a lot of great memories from that tour.

MT: Slash's Snakepit needed a drummer for their 1995 tour. Do you remember getting that phone call?
BT: Yes, Slash's manager is also Zakk's manager so it was very simple. When he needed a drummer, his manager knew that Zakk wasn't working with Pride & Glory, so they just called me. I went down and jammed with Slash, and I guess a few other drummers came down, and that was it.

MT: Slash was still in Guns N' Roses at that point. What would he share with the Snakepit guys about Guns and Axl?
BT: I recorded all of the dirt that the world wants to know. I have it all. And I am saving it.

MT: Share a little of it?
BT: I can't. No. It's too big. This will change the world…maybe even the galaxy. Nah, Nah. (laughs). I really wasn't worried about it. I am a fan of Gun N' Roses, and I was enjoying my time playing with Slash, who is one of my favorite rock guitar players of all time. I never once asked a question about Guns N' Roses. I didn't care. It was a huge band that had internal drama. So do a million other bands, you know?

MT: Slash discussed the Snakepit tour in his book, *Slash*, saying, "For the first time in years, touring was very easy, my band mates were loads of fun and low on drama, and every gig was about playing rock and roll." Did you feel the same way?
BT: 100 percent. He said it better than I could have. It wasn't Guns N' Roses, we weren't selling millions of CDs during that time, but it was a solid rock band doing solid rock shows. I was a hired gun to do a job, and I was very proud to be there.

MT: A few years later in 1998, you joined Foreigner. Around this time, long-time Foreigner singer, Lou Gramm, had surgery on a benign brain tumor. Upon his return to the band, he struggled with his weight, stamina, and voice. What do you recall from being in the band at that time?
BT: When I came into the band and was at my first rehearsal that was the first time that anyone had been in the same room with Lou since his surgery. Lou did have a bit of a struggle. It was a whole new world for this guy. Here is one of the most bad ass singers in rock, trying to duplicate what he had done 20 years before, after all of this stuff he just went through. It's not normal. Most people are just happy to wake up and be alive, and here is this guy wanting to sing these tough songs like, "I Want to Know What Love is," and "Feels Like the First Time," and "Hot Blooded." If you didn't know the whole story, it might be easy to be critical of his performances. But for me, it was awesome.

MT: Foreigner opened for Journey on that tour in 1999. Any good stories?
BT: One night, right before Foreigner went on, the Journey guys came up to me and said, "Deen (Castronovo) injured himself. Can you play?"

222

I said, "Okay." They asked me whose set I wanted to use; mine or Dean's? I said, "Don't use mine. It says Foreigner on it!" After the Foreigner set, I jumped off stage and ran into the Journey dressing room, and I was trying to write some notes to myself, but the manager was like, "C'mon, we have to go on. We're going to get dinged for curfews, overtimes, blah, blah, blah." Remember, we are playing in front of 17,000 people, and I have never played most of the songs in Journey's set. So, I jumped up on stage with Journey and I went for it. I made some train wreck mistakes up there, but at the end of the day, I did most of it okay. That was *thee* number one, undisputed, most challenging gig that I have played.

Brian in the groove. Las Vegas, April 2012.
Photo by Harold Mountain.

MT: After playing with Foreigner, you played with Ozzy during Ozzfest 2000. Was it Zakk that recommended you?
BT: No, it wasn't. I learned that Ozzy's drummer, who was Mike Bordin at the time, was committed to another gig during the Ozzfest dates. I was sitting in LA thinking, "I know too many people in this camp. It would be a travesty if I couldn't at least get an audition." So, I just started making phone calls. It was (Robert) Trujillo or Joe Holmes who called me back. They asked me to come down, and we played a couple songs. They then asked me to come back when Sharon and Ozzy were there later that day. I did, and they asked me to come back

three days later for the final audition. When I got the gig, I was also mixing and recording my band, Ball's record so I started doubling up with that, and Oz rehearsals. It was intense and fun!

MT: Do you recall what song you auditioned with?
BT: I think that it was "War Pigs".

MT: What state of mind was Ozzy in at that time? Did he hang with the band?
BT: I didn't have anything to compare it to, but Ozzy was Ozzy. He came to rehearsal when he was supposed to, he'd hang around, bullshit with us for a while, go home, come back, sing, bullshit with us, you know? He was pretty straight forward. He's a character, but he didn't come in and bite the head off a bat or anything. He seemed focused, and straight up.

MT: You then toured with the great Glenn Hughes in 2001. What is Glenn like?
BT: Glenn was a pleasure to work with. He is high energy. He gets on a mic with his bass, and it's an avalanche of groove and melody. He is such an inspiration, because there is so much intense energy. His singing is amazing, his playing is amazing and he can play for hours without stopping. He had great Bonzo stories. I love John Bonham, and those two were buds. So, it was nice to hear him throw out comparisons of my drumming to Bonzo. We had a good time. It was a lot of fun.

MT: In 2001, you joined forces with Billy Idol, not only as a drummer, but as a song writer until 2009. How did you and Billy hook up?
BT: We did a couple of summer tours in 2001 and 2002. Then in 2003, we had just finished up another summer tour, and our bass player mentioned that I had a studio down the street, and that Billy and I should go jam a bit. It was that simple. We wrote a tune one day, hit it off, and kept writing.

MT: How did the publishing work with Billy?
BT: Yeah, he took everything and he laughed at me. When he gets checks, he actually makes photocopies of them and sends them to me and writes, "HA, HA! You get nothing, HA HA!" and I just say, "Thank you for giving me the chance, Billy." NO! (laughs). He is a very simple guy. He loves music, and he loves rock 'n' roll. If he is having fun, then everything is cool. He doesn't need the drama. So, if

we are in a room together writing, and the end result is a song, it's a co-write. We're splitting it.

MT: During a break in 2005, you toured with Velvet Revolver for three weeks as Matt Sorum had injured his hand. Did Slash call you directly for that gig?
BT: No. Slash says if you want to be friends, then you have to first accept calls from my people. So there is a string of people I have to go through and I tell them, "I would love to talk to Slash. He's the best, I love him," and then they put him on the phone. (laughs). No! Slash just called me up and asked me, "What are you doing? Can you do this?" I didn't think that I could, because I was on a tight schedule with Billy Idol. I revisited my schedule, called him back and said, "I think I can make this happen." I made notes for a couple nights after the Billy Idol shows listening to their set list. Later that week, I flew into LAX, took a cab straight to rehearsal, jumped on a kit, and started playing with the guys.

MT: Did Matt really hurt his hand in a boating accident?
BT: He came to our Las Vegas show and he had a wrap on his hand. I thought that he injured one of his fingers water skiing.

MT: During 2006-07 you would fill in for Jason Bonham while Foreigner was touring. What happened to Jason at the time?
BT: It was really simple. He loves motorcycling and he hurt himself. Have you noticed I do a lot of fill-ins for injured drummers?! Foreigner was going to be pissed, so Jason called me to see if I was available to fill in. If I was, he could call Mick Jones a little more calmly and tell him that I could do the gig. I took the gig, and that's how this all started in 2006. Jason was actually there on the road with us. He would sing backing vocals on a song sometimes near the end of the show. Then in 2007, that was a totally different deal. There were several shows that Jason was called away for, including the Led Zeppelin reunion. While he was away rehearsing or touring, I was still with Billy, but would also fill in for Jason with Foreigner. The coolest thing that happened out of all of this is to be able to sit here and tell you, right now, that I have officially opened for Led Zeppelin! We played one song at the 02 Arena - the Ahmet Ertegun tribute. We were the band that played the song before Zeppelin came on stage, so technically, I opened for Zeppelin! And that rules so hard!

MT: In early 2010, you joined Lynch Mob. What is your relationship with George like?

BT: I can't stand him. He calls me too much. He is annoying basically. (laughs). George is awesome. I was doing a NAMM-type jam session after the show, along with Robbie Crane. We were the rhythm section, playing with different guitar players over a couple of days. One night it was Tracii Guns and George Lynch. We had crossed paths before, but we had never jammed together. So we had a good time, and he called me a while later and asked me if I wanted to join Lynch Mob. I was committed, but later I got to squeeze in a couple of dates with him and we started a relationship. It's been two or three years, and it's now led to T&N.

MT: Tell us about T&N with the Dokken guys. Are you or Mick Brown going to be playing drums?

BT: That's an open-ended thing, and let's add some more fun to this. I have completed my drum parts on nine of 12 tracks on the new Dokken record, and will finish the next three this week. What the hell! We'll add a little more drama to the mix!

MT: Are you referring to T&N? (Tooth and Nail, with George, Jeff Pilson, and Mick Brown)

BT: No, I'm talking about Don Dokken. The new Dokken record that I am the drummer on. (laughs). I don't know when the record is coming out, but I am the drummer on it. It wasn't intentional, it's just that a couple other guys were unavailable and they called me as I am friends with the guys in the band.

MT: I didn't know this. Mick and Don are no longer close?

BT: Nobody knows it! No, no. Mick and Don are close and Mick still plays with Dokken, but it's more of a scheduling thing. Mick is now touring with Ted Nugent. The same thing happened with the last Dokken album. Another drummer played on that one too.

MT: Jumping back to June of 2010, you learned you would be drumming for the legendary band, Whitesnake. Who told you that you had the gig?

BT: David Coverdale did. A buddy of Glenn Hughes's and David's saw me play with Glenn, and he had told David about me years before. So, when David put Whitesnake back together in 2003, he had gotten a hold of me and I had sent him some video stuff of me with Ozzy, Foreigner and Billy Idol. He dug it, but he was also waiting to see if

Tommy Aldridge was available. David and I talked, Tommy became available, and that was it. But, I was in Billy (Idol), and really happy there. Years later in 2010, I jammed with Doug Aldrich at a benefit show. We hit it off. A few months later, Doug and David were talking and wanted to get a new drummer ready. They had the record ready to go, and it was that simple. They called me and said, "Here is our plan. We're doing a new record. We want you to play drums on it, and join the band. We're not touring till 2011." It was really enticing and worked perfectly for me, because I just got home from the Foreigner tour and wanted to spend some time at home and with my kids. A couple weeks later in May, we worked everything out. We did the record in June, and then we toured all 2011.

MT: How much flexibility does David Coverdale give you in playing the classics?
BT: He gives me 100 percent flexibility as long as I don't abuse the privilege! David was like, "Make it sound good and have fun." He would say, "Tichmeister, I want you to be Brian Tichy in this band." He doesn't want me to be Tommy Aldridge or Cozy or Ian. There is a certain amount of trust there, which I think is the key thing.

With The Zep Set in Las Vegas April 2012.
Photo by Harold Mountain.

MT: Not long after you joined Whitesnake, you decided to put together a tribute for one of your big influences.

BT: In between tours in 2010, I realized it was coming up on the 30-year anniversary of John Bonham's passing. Being that he is my favorite drummer, I thought that he should get a proper tribute from some of the drummers that he influenced. There are so many of us. The idea was to simply put a replica drum set on stage of his most popular kit, the amber vistalite Ludwigs, have every drummer involved pick their favorite Led Zeppelin song, and have the band, The Moby Dicks, (laughs) serve as the house band. Michael Devin, Whitesnake's bass player, came up with the name. It's the best name ever for a band! Then, I started calling drummers. At first I was thinking we do it in a rehearsal room and videotape it. Then I involved my friend, Joe Sutton, who promotes around town. He locked in September 25 for us at the Key Club. Setting it up became a full time job, but it was awesome! We did the event without any corporate sponsorship at all. We had 18 drummers there, as well as the Bonham family. Jason played. So did Steven Adler, Simon Wright, Frankie Banali, Vinnie Appice, Bobby Blotzer. The list was huge. We just had a two-day rehearsal and did the gig. We did it again a few months later in January with Xavier Muriel, Dave Lombardo, Jason Sutter and many others. Deborah Bonham got up and sang with Khurt Maier from Salty Dog! It was amazing, and there are many awesome videos of the night on YouTube. We also just announced "Bonzo's Birthday Bash." It is on his 64th birthday on May 31st in Hollywood at the House of Blues. Some guys are back, and some new guys are in; Portnoy, Luzier, Donati, Mayorga, Luccketta Sorum, and it's growing. It is the coolest show I have ever been a part of!

MT: In 2011, you started Something Unto Nothing (S.U.N.) with Sass Jordan. It's a great project in which you actually play guitar. You have been in the studio, and recently toured. What are the plans for S.U.N.?

BT: We are finally looking at securing a record deal. It's a real fun thing for me to write with Sass, as she is one of my best friends now. I always look forward to working with her whether we are writing or performing. We need a deal. We need a label to get behind us and make people aware, so that we can go out and play and kick ass, and see if it sticks.

MT: We just briefly touched on your career, but you have participated in other projects involving Steven Tyler, Seether, Ace Frehley, Gilby Clarke, Jack Blades, Kenny Wayne Shepperd, Richie Kotzen, and Tommy Shaw, to name a few. Do you have a favorite experience outside of what we have discussed?
BT: All those guys are great. They are awesome players and great people, and I hope that I get to work with them all again. But, the coolest - just because it was a little bit surreal - was being the drummer on Steven Tyler's first-ever solo single. While I tracked that drum track, he sat in the control room behind the window watching. I am a hardcore Aerosmith fan. My first record was *Live! Bootleg*, and I love everything about that record. But, to have Steven Tyler sit there and watch me play drums to a song? It was just a simple drum track, but he's a drummer. I am expecting him to tell me what to do. We walked through it the night before, then I came in that morning and I played it through once. Steven says, "You gotta snare with a little more ring to it. Like a piccolo snare or somethin'?" I went and got my snare, but I knew it was a little lower sounding. So I cranked the skin real tight, and I hit it off to the side to get a high pitch. We did the same track again with the new snare, and they called me in the control room. I walked in. Steven turns around and says, "You're a great fuckin' drummer. Very definitive." I was like, "Holy Shit!" And we were done. Second take and that was it.

MT: You recently were featured as a guest drummer on "That Metal Show" in April 2012. How long does it take to film an episode?
BT: We filmed two episodes in one day. With set up time and everything, I was probably there 11:00 am to 7:00 pm.

MT: Is the show a big party?
BT: No. It's a great bunch of people and everyone there was so positive. I had a great time. The day I was there, we had Scott Ian, Slash, Jack Russell, the guys from T&N and Alice Cooper, so I was hanging out with friends. It's TV, so everything is on a very tight schedule.

MT: You debuted your Speed Bag Drum Kit on the show. When did you get into hitting the speed bag?
BT: I started hitting the speed bag in September of 2008. I have been trying to incorporate the speed bag as part of my drum kit since 2009, with Foreigners blessing. Before I even started hitting the speed bag, I

thought it made sense. It's controlled chaos and it's percussive. The more you hit the bag in time, the more technique is involved. Foreigner was going to allow it on the stage during my solo. I had a platform made for the bag that we tried one night at sound check. It was too bulky, too heavy, and too much to ask the crew to throw on my drum set for 30 seconds each night. Same thing with Whitesnake. For That Metal Show, I was just going to play the drums. Then I was approached by Balazs Boxing. They produce some killer boxing gear. They had seen some YouTube footage of me hitting the bag, and wanted to partner in some way. I had just got the gig to play on the show, so I asked Balazs to build me a platform that was sturdy enough to allow me to play the drums and hit the speed bag at the same time. Balazs made me this bad ass platform, and the timing couldn't have been better. When I told the VH1 people what I wanted to do, they were like, "Cool!" To them it's entertainment. Everything *just* fit on the platform, and the end result was something that I had been thinking about for years. On another note, ESPN has contacted me about doing something tying in the speed bag and drums on a show with them as well.

MT: After reading Modern Drummer for so many years, how did it feel to be nominated in their Reader's Poll for 2012?
BT: Finally! A check that I wrote to somebody went to good use! (laughs) No, it was awesome. I wasn't expecting that. Jason Bonham, Chad Smith, Taylor Hawkins, and Travis Barker are all very popular drummers in very big bands. I am the underdog drummer in that group, and I am sure most drummers are saying, "who?" All I cared about was that somebody thought of me enough to put my name on that list. That alone is bad ass!

MT: You have played with many of the best metal guitar players in the world. Who has impressed you the most?
BT: There's not one. They are all awesome. Vinnie Moore, Zakk Wylde, Slash, Steve Stevens, Stevie Salas, Mick Jones, Joe Holmes, Doug Aldrich, Reb Beach, George Lynch. They are all different, and I have learned something from all of them. That is a bunch of bad ass guitar players right there! Seriously! I am looking at that list and if they all played a festival together, you would have some of the best the world has heard!

MT: Excluding Whitesnake, is there a hard rock band you would jump at the opportunity to drum for?
BT: Not many people know this band, but if I could be the drummer for these guys everything would be complete. It's Page, Plant, and Jones I think. That's it. A little band called Led Zeppelin. I know that is Jason's drum chair, but I would be a liar if I didn't say that is the number one drum chair in the world. Paul McCartney would be another one, as well as Heart. I love Michael DeRosier, and I love Ann and Nancy Wilson, and Roger Fisher. I just love that band. I can't forget Kiss either. They were my first band I got into.

MT: If you were asked to do MTV's Cribs, would you do it?
BT: Of course. I always have room in one of my mansions for stuff like that! We take the golf carts around the lakes and water ski, and you pick which butler you want to serve you that day!

MT: How big is your current place you call home?
BT: Bigger than most, not as big as some. About 2400 square feet.

MT: What kind of car do you own?
BT: An SUV, a Yukon.

MT: Over the years, what gig has benefited you the most financially?
BT: Billy Idol.

MT: Are you registered to vote? Will you be voting in November (2012)? Who for?
BT: Yes, yes, and I am undecided.

MT: What current band mates do you hang out with the most?
BT: Michael Devin and George Lynch.

MT: Do you smoke cigarettes?
BT: No.

MT: What was your drug of choice back in the day?
BT: Just your basic drinking.

MT: If you took a drug test today, what would it tell us?
BT: That I drink beer.

MT: Should marijuana be legalized?
BT: Why not?

MT: Do you follow sports?
BT: No, but I follow MMA and boxing a bit.

MT: Craziest groupie story?
BT: I will tell you the best story that I can't top, but it really doesn't involve me. You know Sweet Connie from the "Grand Funk" song, "American Band"? She is immortalized in that song, and she was known as one of the biggest groupies ever. Back in the day when I was touring with Vinnie Moore, she showed up at a club and totally went after our bass player after our gig at a diner. She was so forward with him. I think the end result was that he did mess around with her just to say that he did. We were like in our early 20's, and here is Little Rock Connie who has been around since the 70s. I just remember being turned off by everything that she represented, but I believe our bass player took advantage of it. I mean, I personally don't have really good stories.

MT: What is the coolest backyard party you have played over the years?
BT: You know, I played in Eddie Van Halen's backyard with him at a party once. He was in a different state of mind back then in 2006. It was amazing. It was a big party in his back yard for an adult film that he had done some music for. He hired us as a cover band, and he got up and jammed with us. It was amazing just to jam with Eddie and be at his house. Even just goofing around in his backyard you could tell how talented this guy is. Eddie's groove is an unstoppable force! It's so powerful, you basically just jump into it and roll with it. To play with such a mighty player with a groove so fat and universally pleasing was something that I am glad to have experienced in this life time, no shit! He talked with us for a while as well. He told us about some stuff from road. Just some quickie stories. That was a great night. You can actually see footage on youtube from it. It was amazing.

MT: Who have you been listening to in your car?
BT: Led Zeppelin, Rush, and Fever Ray. They are from Sweden.

MT: What beverage do you drink during a show?
BT: Water and a couple of lite beers.

MT: Who are you currently endorsed by?
BT: Natal Drums, Paiste Cymbals, Regal Tip drum sticks featuring, "Tish Sticks," Remo Heads, Intex guitar cables, Dunlop accessories, and Presonus preamps.

MT: When is the last time you paid for a cymbal?
BT: I believe it was 1987.

MT: Have you ever been afraid for your safety while on stage performing?
BT: At Donington with Pride & Glory in 1994. It was my first time there. 60,000 people. Everyone warns you about the bottles of piss that are going to be pelting you. People will drink a beer or water, and rather than try to get to a rest room, they just piss in the bottle and throw it on stage. I didn't get hit by any bottles of piss, but that was for sure going on.

MT: Who is the one person that you run into knowing you're going to have a long night of partying ahead of you?
BT: Vinnie Paul.

MT: When was the last time you were blown away by a band's live performance?
BT: Cool question. Let me really think about this. Pantera. Every time I have seen them! And, you cannot deny the power of a Phish concert! Or Rage Against The Machine! Or James Brown! Or the Allman's!

MT: The best rock album ever made?
BT: Led Zeppelin, *Physical Graffiti*.

MT: What advice would you provide to a player who wants to play rock music for a living?
BT: If you are not obsessed, possessed and in love with it, don't bother.

MT: What are you working on now? How can people get a hold of you?
BT: Please check out www.somethinguntonothing.com and Something Unto Nothing on Facebook. Also www.briantichy.com and Brian Tichy on Facebook.

Acknowledgments

Jennifer Todorov: The most understanding, supportive, and encouraging person I know. Jennifer assisted me in too many ways to mention here, and I could never thank her enough. I am an incredibly lucky guy, and everyone who knows her tells me this regularly. She is truly amazing.

Erik Luftglass: He runs one of the best boutique music management companies in the country, and has opened numerous doors for me along the way. Watch for some of the talent coming out of The ESL Music Group, including Mike Portnoy's new project, Adrenaline Mob. I have known Erik since his days at VH1, and I feel fortunate to call him a good friend.

Tim Shiner: Tim is one of the most driven guys I know, and one of the best business coaches in the country. The moment I start losing direction or motivation, Tim can get me back on track in minutes. He helped in critiquing every interview as I did them, and assisted me in fine tuning the process. His generosity never ceases to amaze people, myself included. I have learned a lot from Tim over the last 15 years, and will continue to do so in the years to come.

Jay Reynolds and Jeff Duncan: Like most new projects, people are hesitant to be the first ones to jump on board. Jay and Jeff were not only not hesitant, but excited about the project when I pitched them at NAMM in January 2012. I'll never forget standing out on the convention center balcony in Anaheim freezing as Jay smoked a cigarette. He listened to me for five minutes, took a puff of his cigarette, extended his hand, and said. "Let's do it, dude. I'm in!" Jeff confirmed with me at NAMM as well, and called me just days later. Thanks guys! I'm proud of the book and hope that you will be too.

The Photographers: Over 50 photos were used in the book, from 25 different photographers. The photographers shared some of their amazing work with me, and allowed me to print their art in the book. It was a very generous thing to do, and I am appreciative.

Rob and Philly Joe at Ride for Dime: When I was searching for a non-profit organization to partner with, Rob and Philly made everything very easy and seamless. The Ride for Dime organization is blowing up, and I am proud that the book is providing a portion of the proceeds to further musical education to America's youth.

John VanOphem: How many people like their lawyer? I do! As busy as John gets, he answers the phone when I call, or will call me back in minutes if he can't take my call. He has been extremely helpful in establishing all of my IP items, and I know that our high school friendship will continue for decades.

Kyle Markman: Kyle is a marketing whiz who continues to toss good ideas my way regarding the marketing of the book. I had a minor setback during the writing process, and Kyle turned it into a marketing gem in a couple minutes.

Others: Taylor Carlson with Rock Society Radio, Andrew Babcock with Hair Metal Mansion, Nancy Orsini-Princi and Claudia Moreira with Global Onslaught, Brian Dycus with Hard Rock Nights, Dalila Kriheli with Rock Star Pix, Jenny Modglin with The RSE Group, Harold Mountain, Tommy and Kristie Regits from Off the Rails Music School, Darren Upton, Mark Hyska, Cheryl Smydra, Sheila Schultz Miller and Marianne Thompson. You all made life much easier for me, and I appreciate your support from the very early stages of the project.

Lastly, but certainly not least, the participants. The time that you all spent with me exchanging emails, phone calls, and the interview itself was incredibly generous. The process was something that I will not forget, and I am very appreciative. I hope that you had half of the fun that I had reliving some of the past during our interviews. I can't thank you all enough.